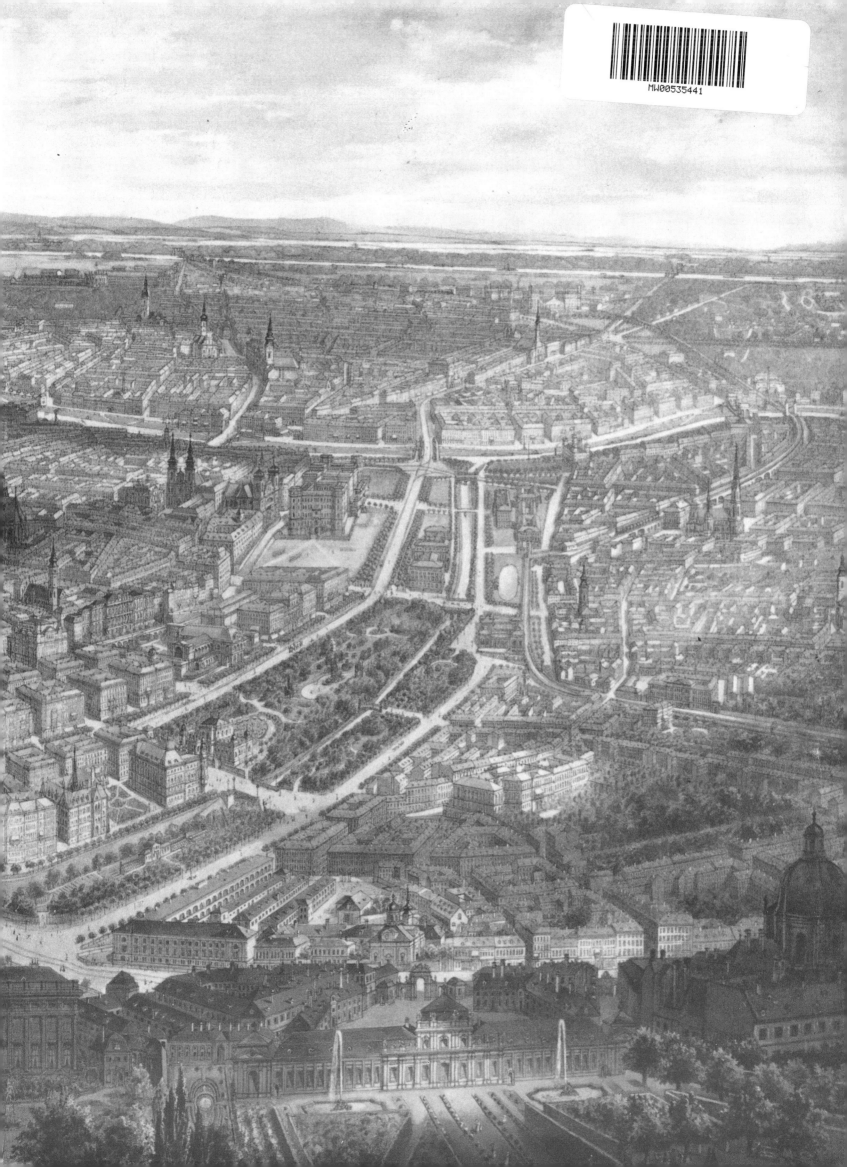

PALACES OF VIENNA

PALACES OF VIENNA

Wolfgang Kraus • Peter Müller

The Vendome Press • New York

Published in the United States of America in 1993 by
The Vendome Press, 515 Madison Avenue, New York, NY 10022

Distributed in the United States and Canada by
Rizzoli International Publications
300 Park Avenue South, New York, NY 10010

Design by Reinhard Fuchs

Library of Congress Cataloging-in-Publication Data
Kraus, Wolfgang, 1958—
        [Wiener Palais. English]
        The palaces of Vienna / Wolfgang Kraus and Peter Müller.
        P.cm.
        ISBN 0–86565–132–9
        1. Palaces—Austria—Vienna. 2. Architecture, Domestic—
Austria—Vienna—Themes, motives. 3. Vienna (Austria—Buildings,
structures etc. I. Müller, Peter, 1947—   . II. Title.
NA7720.K7313   1993
728.88280943613—dc20   93–11113
                                                                    CIP

Printed and bound in Italy

CONTENTS

Introduction **7**

Town Palais

The Hofburg **18**

The Archbishop's Palace **28**

Palais Starhemberg **32**

Palais Lobkowicz **36**

Palais Liechtenstein **42**

Palais Harrach **50**

Palais Mollard-Clary **54**

Palais Esterházy **58**

The Winter Palais of Prince Eugene **62**

Palais Caprara **70**

Palais Batthyány-Schönborn **74**

Palais Daun-Kinsky **78**

Palais Neupauer-Breuner **84**

Palais Fürstenberg **88**

Palais Erdödy-Fürstenberg **92**

Palais Rottal **94**

Palais Dietrichstein **100**

Palais Fries-Pallavicini **102**

The Albertina **108**

Palais Modena **114**

Palais Coburg **118**

Garden Palais

Favorita "Collegium Theresianum" **122**

The Liechtenstein Garden Palais **128**

Schloss Hetzendorf **134**

Schloss Schönbrunn **140**

Augartenpalais **148**

Palais Schwarzenberg **152**

Palais Strozzi **160**

Palais Schönburg **162**

Palais Schönborn **164**

Palais Auersperg **168**

Palais Trautson **174**

The Belvedere **180**

Palais Rasumofsky **192**

Palais Clam-Gallas **196**

Palais Metternich **198**

Ringstrasse Palais

Palais Todesco **204**

Palais Württemberg **208**

Palais Schey **212**

Archduke Ludwig Viktor's Palais **214**

Archduke Wilhelm's Palais **218**

Palais Larisch **222**

Palais Lützow **224**

Palais Epstein **226**

Palais Henckel-Donnersmarck **230**

Palais Ephrussi **232**

Palais Falkenstein **236**

Palais Rothschild **238**

Introduction

Vienna can boast a wealth of palaces matched by few other cities in the world. Indeed, the palace – or palais, as the Viennese call it – remains an integral part of the Austrian capital's urbanscape, despite the loss of many palatial dwellings to social and economic change, war, and speculative building. (In English, most of the palais to be seen here would be known by more modest terms, such as "mansion" or "town house.") Generally built as the residence of a royal or at least an aristocratic family, the palais is an impressive structure conveying a sense of affluence, aesthetic sophistication, and social rank. Vienna owes the profusion of these masterpieces of secular architecture to its having long been the seat of powerful sovereigns, first the Holy Roman and then the Austrian Emperors. In addition, the Imperial or Habsburg court made the city a magnet for noble families from all parts of the Empire, as well as from other European countries. This was particularly true during the Baroque period – the 17th and 18th centuries – which proved to be a golden age in Austrian history, giving rise to many new Viennese palais, unique in their number, concentration, and quality.

The decimation of this great architectural heritage in the course of the last 150 years has been caused by a variety of factors. Splendid settings and Baroque ostentation forfeited all raison d'Étre once their foundations in society crumbled. Later generations deemed the Baroque palais too burdened with useless decoration for the urgent practical needs of modern life. The Baroque style quite simply fell out of favor, its enormous spaces having come to seem a shameless extravagance. This shift in taste had its most devastating effect upon the garden palais. The tremendous urban expansion that continued throughout the 19th century created an almost insatiable demand for more living space, which made the large, elaborate gardens appear ripe for redevelopment. Today some 80 percent of the 400 or so palais that once encircled the heart of old Vienna have been stripped of both their vast gardens and their imaginative architectural features.

Vienna's town palais, on the other hand, proved more adaptable to modern purposes. Even as they were increasingly abandoned by private families, the great houses satisfied the requirements of a constantly growing bureaucracy, which thereby ensured their survival. Already in the late 18th century, Empress Maria Theresia could decide to convert Prince Eugene's winter palais of 1695-98 into an office building. Today, a raft of ministries and official bodies have their headquarters in some of Vienna's most historic and prestigious palais. The palais around the Ring, erected only in the second half of the 19th century, have long since lost their function as residences for a recently ennobled bourgeoisie. Indeed, their transformation into office blocks, government buildings, or hotels led to massive destruction of not only interiors but original structures as well. At the same time, however, the Imperial palaces, despite the absence of a court and its ceremonial ways, have preserved their traditional appearance and, for that every reason, constitute tourist attractions of the highest order.

The history of how Vienna came to be settled and then developed into a major city can be clearly read from an aerial photograph or a street plan. The castrum, or military encampment, established by the Romans at the end of the 1st century AD survived to become the core of the later metropolis. A thousand years later, Vienna emerged as the seat of the Babenberg Dukes and thereupon experienced its first golden age. Now, as the city grew beyond the framework of a Roman encampment, it assumed the structure characteristic of medieval towns, such as can still be found all over Central Europe. The Church of St. Stephen and the Scottish monastery gave witness to the rank Vienna held as the residence of a sovereign Prince. The town fortifications also underwent new construction, on a scale so generous that it would permit the 19th-century Habsburgs to expand the city within the walls' defensive ring.

It was Ottokar II, the King of Bohemia and heir to the Babenbergs, who, in 1275, laid the foundation stone

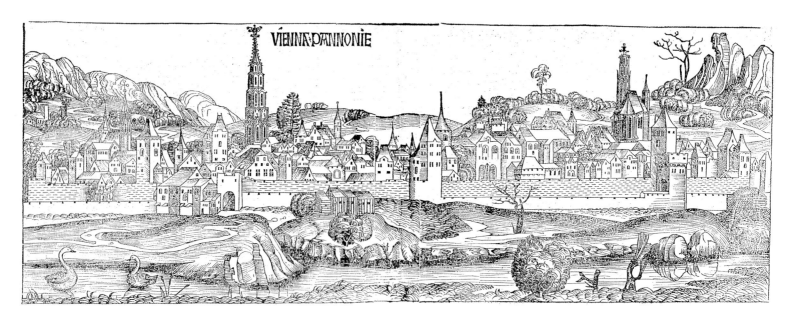

Fifteenth-century Vienna from the north. Woodcut from Weltchronik by H. Schedel, 1493.

for the building that would become the Hofburg. A year later, Vienna fell to Germany's Rudolph von Habsburg, the Holy Roman Emperor who soon thereafter placed his son Albrecht on the throne of Austria.

By the mid-15th century Vienna was characterized by numerous ecclesiastical buildings as well as by the stately houses of prosperous burghers, a setting that reflected the importance and power of both the clergy and the middle classes. The earliest known description of Vienna dates from that era, a statement composed in 1438 by Silvio Piccolomini, subsequently Pope Pius II: "Vienna is enclosed by a peripheral wall that is two thousand paces long; it has important outskirts that are surrounded by broad moats and walls. But also the city itself has a mightly moat and in front of it a very high wall. Behind the ditch comes the thick, tall ramparts with numerous towers and outworks such as are appropriate for defense." In 1485 Antonio de Bonfini evinced great enthusiasm for Vienna in a topographical work prepared for Matthias Corvinus, King of Hungary: "The actual city lies like a palace in the midst of its surrounding suburbs"; moreover, he wrote, Vienna belonged "certainly amongst the finest cities of the barbarians."

The independent, flourishing, and self-confident bourgeoisie – particularly the outward-looking traders and merchants – set the style of the city. Their tall, narrow houses functioned as both private residences and places of business. The deep, vaulted cellars beneath them provided additional storage space for wine and others goods, becoming ever-more useful as the urban scene grew increasingly crowded. Rising high above the compact mass of dwellings were the spires and towers of numerous churches and monastic complexes.

Vienna's glory as a bourgeois town ended abruptly in the first half of the 16th century. Disaster first struck in 1525 with the fire that ravaged almost half the city. Then, a year later, the burghers lost practically all their powers through a new city ordinance abolishing their old rights and placing Vienna under the power of the reigning Prince. Next, in 1529, came the fateful siege laid by the Ottoman Turks, whose attack would be repulsed but without relieving Vienna of an ongoing Turkish threat. As a consequence, stagnation set in for the next 150 years, keeping the town in a constant state of anxiety about the adequacy of its defenses. Ferdinand I, who transferred the Imperial court and most of its administration permanently to Vienna, decided to construct new, state-of-the-art fortifications. To this end, he summoned Europe's most important specialists. The defensive works, which absorbed vast amounts of both materials and manpower, impeded all other building activity for many years. How far Vienna fell behind other European towns could be determined by the sovereign's own residence, which, even after enlargement and reconstruction in relatively contemporary style, could not conceal its character as a medieval fortress. The massive rectangular enclosure, with its battlements, corner towers, and encircling moat, had to satisfy the monarch's needs. Clearly, Vienna had become a backward, impoverished, and neglected place. In this unfavorable political and economic climate, a situation exacerbated by the religious conflict of the Reformation, Europe's rebirth – the Renaissance – would have little impact upon the physical appearance of heavily bastioned Vienna. Nevertheless, the Stallburg was erected during the reign of Ferdinand, followed by Neugebèude Castle outside the city gates in the reign of Maximilian II.

Ferdinand had the Stallburg constructed adjacent to the old fortress as a palace for his son Maximilian, recently returned from Habsburg-dominated Spain. When the heir ascended the throne as Maximilian II, he moved into the Hofburg, leaving his unfinished residence to serve as the court stables. Still, the Stallburg, with its three-story, arcaded courtyard, would emerge as the most important Renaissance structure in Vienna.

Maximilian, who had grown up in Spain, was keenly receptive to all the new developments in art, science, and the intellectual life. In keeping with his contemporary, humanistic views and his enthusiasm for the brilliant artistic innovations of Italy, the new Emperor sought to embody his self-image as a Renaissance Prince in an important building. Thus, it was in 1569 that work started on the Neugebèude ("New Building") to the southeast of the town, in what is now the Simmering quarter of modern Vienna. Not until 1587, however, would the gigantic project see completion, under the Italian architect Pietro Ferrabosco during the reign of Rudolf II. The very name Neugebèude signaled a departure from old traditions such as those found in the nearby Imperial hunting lodge at Ebersdorf.

Indeed, the Neugebèude introduced a new, expansive world into the narrow confines of remote Vienna. The choice of site, the unusually large dimensions, the immense cost of the dÄcor and statuary, the layout of the opulent gardens, the charmingly extravagant fountains, the exotic plants and animals – all this luxury left the Viennese in a state of utter amazement. Today, the bare walls that survive in the Neugebèude scarcely suggest the former splendor of the structure, once considered the biggest and most important villa suburbana north of the Alps. Here the Emperor had succeeded in enlarging his artistic interests beyond mere collecting to include monumental architecture.

Insufficient space forced Rudolf II to undertake a further expansion of the Hofburg. The Emperor had Ferrabosco replace the old Cillier Court with a independent, quadrangular block. The so-called "Rudolph Building" – now known as the Amalienburg – was then decorated and furnished by a permier team of Italian artists, whose work, however, would subsequently undergo considerable alteration.

remained absent from Vienna, preferring to focus their attentions upon their own estates, great or small, and to enjoy a largely independent life where they were lords of all they surveyed. The high nobility did indeed participate in the sessions and councils of the provincial diets, but the rest of the landed aristocracy avoided urban life as far as possible. This tendency to flee the city was a phenomenon of the period, when country life and the study of nature became central concerns and hunting a favorite pastime.

Like the Renaissance before it, Baroque art made its way to Vienna from Italy, where it had originated in Rome as a logical evolution of the previous style. Unlike the latter, the new art would encounter favorable conditions in Vienna and thus have an effect so profound as to renew the entire face of the capital city.

Vienna's Baroque Age began in the reign of Leopold I with the construction of the so-called "Leopold Block" at the Hofburg. This symbol of the Imperial court's emphasis on ceremony coincided with important changes within the worlds of politics, economics, society, and religion. The campaign undertaken by the monarch to centralize his government and to exercise absolute power, the entrancing solemnity of the Spanish court etiquette practiced by the Habsburgs, the allocation of court offices to members of the nobility – all combined to make Vienna once again attractive to the feudal aristocracy.

As a consequence of Leopold's policies, however, the gulf between the classes widened, advantaging the nobility at the expense of the bourgeoisie. With the resolution of the Reformation/Counter-Reformation conflicts – a pacification encouraged by the ruling house – obstacles to the rise of the aristocracy had been

Neugebèude Castle in the 18th century. Engraving by Johann Adam Delsenbach after Joseph Emanuel Fischer von Erlach.

swept away. Inevitably, the appointment of high nobles to high office transformed Vienna from a middle-class town to a province of the nobility. With the onset of the Counter-Reformation, Vienna had experienced an enormous boom in the construction of religious buildings. Now the feudal lords started planning ambitious secular projects, with no lack of models to base them upon. Among the cities well in advance of Vienna were not only Rome and Paris but also Salzburg in Austria itself. The Archbishop of Salzburg, Wolf Dieterich von Raitenau, had initiated, as early as 1596, the construction of the new Residenz fashioned after a Roman grandee's palazzo. Then, during the early years of the 17th century, the new Salzburg Cathedral was designed by Vincenzo Scamozzi, a pupil of Andrea Palladio. Once the powerful Archbishop turned medieval Salzburg into the "Rome of the North," Italian art went on to dominate the rebuilding of Vienna as well.

The palais constructed by the Dietrichsteins, the Abensperg-Trauns, the Hoyos, the Liechtensteins, the Strattmanns, and the Starhembergs altered the old Viennese townscape beyond recognition. From the still-dominant medieval tradition of the tall, narrow, gabled burgher's house, Vienna stepped forward without transition into a realm characterized by the broad, stately town palace. One new palace could frequently displace as many as five or six burgher dwellings. In a city still tightly huddled within its ring of defensive walls, whose circumference had not changed since the time of the Babenbergs, the new palais seemed absolutely radical in their breadth, which extended through twenty or even thirty bays. At the same time that such a development bespoke luxury, it also served as a supreme statement of power. Prince Karl Eusebius von Liechtenstein, an architectural theorist, wrote in his treatise of 1678: "For what is splendid in a building is length – and the longer, the nobler – for it is most impressive and majestic to see a great number of windows and pillars." The taste of Imperial Vienna, with its vast territorial claims on Italy, rejected French models in favor of Italian ones. "In its buildings," commented Liechtenstein, "Italy surpasses the whole world and thus of such a kind as to be followed more than any other, for their style is beautiful and splendid and majestic."

It was exclusively Italian architects and decorators who prevailed in Vienna – Lucchese, Carlone, Tencala, Rossi, Gabrieli, and Martinelli, among others. However, in many of the Viennese palais, the Roman palazzo evolved into a formal genre all its own, the result of adaptation to local realities, including the wishes of clients. Despite the monotonous rows of identical windows and the massive bulk, the Viennese palais differed from the Roman prototype mainly because of the building materials used – bricks and plaster rather than cut and dressed stone. Further distinctions came with the greater variety of articulation and a vertical thrust added to the bold horizontal extension. In this way the Baroque palazzo acquired a distinctive Austrian accent. And behind the faìades as well, Vienna diverged from the Roman model, following its own instincts. In the Hapsburg capital, Rome's grandezza – its sober, dignified monumentality – grew somewhat profane, more sensual, and, over time, livelier and less rigorous.

When the Baroque arrived in Vienna, it had still to reach its peak. Locally, this came with an event of momentous import, for the whole of Europe as well as for Vienna: the crushing defeat of the Turks outside the Imperial capital in the year 1683. This victory ended the 150-year trauma of ongoing threat, to life itself, and the resulting stagnation on all sides. Vienna's economy and basic stock of housing had not been fully rehabilitated by the early boom in Baroque construction. Now, deliverance from the Turkish menace became the starting point for an energizing string of political and military successes, all accompanied by comparable achievements in art and architecture.

Longing for expression followed in the wake of danger thwarted. The towering artistic accomplishments of this period, which coincided with the "Heroic Age" in Austrian history, flowed from a combination of many sources and forces: the Imperial house, endowed with all the powers of absolute monarchy; an aristocracy that had acquired immense wealth and influence; the exceptional artistic personalities who fortuitously appeared upon the scene; and a population able to take advantage of the favorable economic situation. All these factors contributed towards making Vienna the site of brilliant developments in art and culture rivaling those attained anywhere else at the time. In sum, the old, long-beleaguered city found itself the beneficiary of an epic renewal.

As a cosmopolitan intellectual center, capable of assimilating and reinvigorating the latest artistic currents in Italy, France, and other advanced regions, the Imperial capital grew so compellingly attractive that to own a town palais there became a must for the greatest families of the nobility. The limited availability of space led to a unique concentration of palais architecture, so that 18th-century Vienna emerged a city of palais, obliging the bourgeoisie to relocate their homes in new developments on the outskirts of the city. In 1730, Vienna could count 930 burghers' houses,

The Liechtenstein garden palais in Rossau, with a view towards the belvedere. Painting of c. 1770 by Bernardo Bellotto.

alongside which stood no less than 248 noblemen's residences.

Prince Johann Adam von Liechtenstein called Vienna's unprecedented building mania an addiction. According to Matthias Fuhrmann, writing in 1766, Prince Johann Adam said: ". . . as God in his goodness had endowed him with great means, he devoted 30,000 florins annually to charity, but not for idle beggars who made a profession out of unemployment, but for needy workmen and masons. He built not out of vanity as he was provided anyway with enough dwellings, but it was on account of the poor men who would gladly work but could not always find employment that he had undertaken such a costly building project." The Elector of Mainz, Prince Lothar Franz von Schönborn, on the other hand, declared: "Building is devilish: when one has started with it, one can never stop?"

In contrast to the older style, the high Baroque town palais displays more originality in the articulation of its exterior and a new wealth of architectural vocabulary. Sculpture as a building element also enjoyed a golden age. However, the greatest splendor by far was to be found within the buildings, where the organization of the Baroque palais responded to contemporary needs. Earlier, the desire for ostentation

was gratified mainly on the faìade, but now the interior functioned as the preferred site for audacious self-promotion. This thoroughly Baroque impulse first registered in the extravagantly designed portico, where coats of arms testified to the rank and origin of the owner, while allegorical figures evoked his glorious qualities.

After the vaulted vestibule comes the actual entrance, composed of a broad, impressively grand staircase, a frescoed ceiling, and a plenitude of statuary on the walls and along the balustrades. The stairwell prepares the visitor for the splendor of the halls, galleries, and salons that lie ahead.

Lady Mary Wortley Montagu, the wife of the British Ambassador to Constantinople, stopped in Vienna in 1716. In her letters she depicts the magnificence of the aristocratic houses she discovered there: "They consist usually of a series of eight or ten large rooms, all with inlaid work, doors and windows enriched with sculpture and gilded, and even high officials have furnishings such as elsewhere one would hardly find in the palaces of ruling princes. Their rooms are hung with the finest tapestries from the Low Countries, with monstrously large mirrors in frames of silver or of brilliant glass ornamented with silver,

Japanese tables, rich, heavy chairs, beds etc decorated with window curtains which are of the heaviest damask and almost all with golden fringes or embroidery. Finally, one sees there also splendid paintings, vases of Japanese porcelain, artistic clocks and big candelabras made of crystal. I have also had the honour to be invited to dine by various cavaliers and high officials and to do them justice the taste and magnificence of their tables is fully in accord with their beautiful vessels. More than once I was offered at least five dishes which were all served in silver and were well prepared; these were followed by a dessert in the most beautiful Chinese porcelain."

It is easy to understand the sighing of the noble lords over their passion for building, which did not confine itself to town palais, but extended as well to include big country seats either constructed or reconstructed, together with the various churches patronized by the building nobility. Moreover, Vienna offered a double opportunity for grandiose domestic architecture, since, in addition to town palais, garden palais could also be put up outside the city's fortifications, now that the Turks no longer menaced the region. The villages near the defensive walls had been removed because of the Turkish threat, and their removal had created a broad strip of land that for a long time remained undeveloped, except for orchards and vineyards. In contrast to the cramped inner city, this ring of open country offered superb sites for garden palais conducive to summer dwelling. Lady Mary Wortley Montagu declared herself marvelously impressed by the splendor of the new outskirts: ffuurrzzI have never seen anything so perfect, agreeable and delightful as the suburbs of Vienna. They are very extensive and consist almost entirely of beautiful palaces which are enchanting because of their situation and design." The garden palais differs from the town palais by its greater intimacy and lightness, its less ceremonial and formal lines. The emergence of the Viennese garden palais began with Martinelli's design for the Liechtenstein palais erected in Rossau in 1691. This structure, in which the dominant features are the cubic mass of the main block and the clear, precise articulation of forms, is completely Italian in spirit. However, a generalized spaciousness heralded the advent of a new concept that would attain its complete expression in the High Baroque garden palais. A fully three-dimensional design, with a more dynamic ground plan and faìade, yielded a light, gay, almost dematerialized architecture. The suite of chambers often climaxes in the grand oval or round room with a dome vault beautifully painted in trompe-l'oeil sky effects. The sala terrena provides a graceful transition from the closed reception area to the open one, which is the garden, an essential component of an overall Gesamtkunstwerk or comprehensive work of art.

The Baroque garden is a carefully ordered and systematically designed space that together with the attendant building forms a perfect unity. A sense of amplitude comes from long perspective allÄes of trellises and clipped hedges.

To the right and left of the main axis, which extends that of the palais, lie the richly ornamental and colorful flower beds laid out like carpets or embroideries. In the groves of trees and bushes, the Baroque garden is given to capricious scenic effects, produced by numerous surprises such as bowling greens, mazes, latticed gates, and theaters formed of clipped hedges. Water flowing through cascades, fountains, ponds, stairs, and jets constitutes an important element of the design. Around Vienna ramps and steps overcame the variable terrain. An abundance of statuary brought out the architectonic character of the garden and its "illusionism." The crowning glory of Viennese garden architecture was the belvedere, a light, airy structure providing a decorative focal point at the garden's highest elevation. Orangeries and hothouses, chapels and aviaries completed the architectural ensemble.

The Baroque gardens of Vienna have been almost totally destroyed. For the most part, they gave way to the tremendous growth of the city in the l9th century. The site of the Althans garden palais in Ungargasse, for example, was divided into 32 plots. The surviving remnants show no trace of the art of the Baroque garden. Only at Prince Eugene's Belvedere and at the Habsburgs' Schönbrunn can one find a living record.

Viennese palace architecture reached its apogee in the designs for the Imperial family and for that great hero of 1693, Prince Eugene of Savoy. During the reign of Charles VI, the Hofburg underwent its ultimate transformation from fortress into palace. The Imperial Chancellery, the Court Library, and the Winter Riding School add both majesty and brilliance to the Imperial residence. The new building that would replace Schönbrunn Castle, destroyed by the Turks, was begun under Leopold I.

According to the first design prepared by Johann Bernhard Fischer von Erlach, Schönbrunn would have exceeded Versailles in size and splendor alike. However, the overreaching, even fantastic scheme was to be supplanted by Fischer's second, more modest design and then actually executed. As his summer residence Charles VI preferred "Favorita" in Wieden; moreover, he busied himself with the idea of an Austrian Escorial at Klosterneuburg. Only with the accession of Maria Theresia would the work on

Schönbrunn Palace be brought to happy conclusion, achieved by Nikolaus Pacassi, working on commission from the new Empress.

Prince Eugene of Savoy erected both a town palais – the Winter Palais in Himmelpfortgasse – and a garden palais – the Belvedere – which together count among the most important works of the Austrian Baroque. It was only natural that this exceptional man – courageous and gifted, versatile and cultivated – would detest all half-measures, an attitude that he fully expressed, as owner and joint creator, in his grandiose architectural ventures. He made a public commitment, following his extraordinary military and political successes, to collaborate in the aesthetic reconstruction of Vienna. Proceeding like a polar opposite to the Imperial family, he realized this ambition quite as spectacularly as he did elsewhere. His house architect was Johann Lukas von Hildebrandt, while the Imperial family favored Fischer von Erlach. Competition spurred on these two great form-givers, who emerged among the towering artistic personalities of their time.

Johann Bernhard Fischer von Erlach was born in Graz in 1656. At the age of thirty, following a fifteen-year apprenticeship under Bernini in Rome, he arrived in Vienna, where his unusual gifts rapidly gained renown. He soon found himself employed by the leading noble families. Count Gundacker Althan, the friend of Emperor Charles VI and later Imperial Chief Inspector of Works, was to be his most important mentor. Fischer von Erlach became the architect for all the palais commissioned by the building-mad Count, every one of which has now disappeared. Among Fischer's major works were Schönbrunn, the Court Library, and the Court Stables, all executed for the Imperial family. He made Karlskirche his most important religious work. Fischer was knighted in 1696

The Ceremonial Hall in the Hofburg. Colored lithograph after Rudolf von Alt.

and in 1705 appointed Imperial Chief Engineer. His great achievement lay in transforming Italian dogma into a very dynamic and imaginative personal idiom. His work constitutes a unique synthesis of all the various tendencies in the European Baroque.

Johann Lukas von Hildebrandt came into the world in Genoa in 1668, the son of German parents. Like Fischer, he went to Rome for his training, which in his case occurred under Carlo Fontana. In 1696 he appeared in Vienna, where by 1701 he had been appointed Imperial Engineer. Hildebrandt was knighted in 1720. His most important clients were Prince Eugene and the Counts Schönborn, for whom he designed a garden palais in Vienna and worked on Pommersfelden Palace in Franconia and the Wurzburg Residenz. His major religious buildings include Peterskirche and Piaristenkirche in Vienna as well as Göttweig Monastery in Lower Austria. On account of their lively, floating quality, their delicate wealth of forms, and their varied ornamentation, Hildebrandt's creations have been called masterpieces of "spiritualized matter."

During the reign of Empress Maria Theresia, new intellectual and artistic trends began arriving from Western Europe. Meanwhile, Pacassi, the Empress' trusted architect, rebuilt Schönbrunn. When completed, the palace, especially the dÄcor within, was a masterpiece of Austrian Rococo. This differed from the French both in its greater sobriety and in its more systematic program, even while retaining the Gallic model's refined sensuality and love of chinoiserie.

These trends, slowly absorbed but with lasting effect, discovered a zealous supporter in the reform-minded Emperor Joseph II, Maria Theresia's son and the brother of Marie Antoinette. During his progressive reign, enlightenment and liberalization gained ground, allowing serious thought to replace ostentatious displays of power. This occurred in all spheres, including architecture and garden design. Thus, Neoclassicism, first manifested in the late Baroque era, took deep roots. The palais of this period are few, but their artistic quality is all the more exquisite, even if the cool elegance they embody appears somewhat alien or remote to Austrian sensibilities. The most important practitioners of Neoclassical architecture include Johann Ferdinand Hetzendorf von Hohenberg and Josef Kornhèusel, together with three Frenchmen: Isidor Canevale, Louis von Montoyer, and Pierre Charles de Moreau. Hohenberg created the Gloriette at Schönbrunn and the palais of the Counts Fries in Josefsplatz. Merchant and banking families – like the Fries, nouveaux riches and freshly ennobled – often came forward as the most eager commissioners of Neoclassical palais. For Duke Albert of Sachsen-Teschen, Montoyer reconstructed the Palais Tarouca, at the same time that he also worked for the Habsburgs, adding the splendid Ceremonial Hall to the Hofburg. However, his most important work is the garden palais for the Russian Ambassador, Andrei Kyrillovitsch, Prince Rasumovsky.

In Vienna as well as in the rest of Europe, the revolutionary year of 1848 brought radical changes in the structure of society. The bourgeoisie broke through the old feudal system and shattered the power of the aristocracy. The social and political convulsions that ensued, from the sudden climax of trends long underway, had a stunning effect upon the Viennese townscape, ultimately transforming it more profoundly than at any time since the Baroque period.

In a hand-written note to the Minister of the Interior, published verbatim on the front page of the Wiener Zeitung on Christmas Eve 1857, the young Emperor Franz Joseph decreed the razing of the capital's old "circumvallations and fortifications," for the sake of linking the inner city with the outer districts already incorporated administratively since 1850. The circle of defenses had long served their purpose and the space they occupied in an overcrowded city was desperately needed. The Emperor's note marked the start of a new era, for it triggered contemporary Europe's greatest urban boom and made Vienna once again a world-class city.

Everything augured well for the development of the Ring, the broad belt of cleared land made available for building by the demolition of the circle of defensive ramparts. The monarchy saw the reconstruction of the capital as a splendid opportunity to draw attention from the recent political chaos and to demonstrate its own reserves of strength. For the bourgeoisie too, the great urban project represented a golden opportunity, allowing them to display their newly acquired rank. And the revolutionaries as well perceived advantages, a chance to convert hard-won rights into structures serving the educational, cultural, and social needs of a budding democracy.

The old nobility withdrew more and more into their town palais and country seats, conscious of their social position and their role as exemplars, but also aware of their declining political influence. With few exceptions, the aristocracy stood aloof and barricaded against the rising tide of social change. Meanwhile, the high bourgeoisie exerted every effort to break down the barriers between themselves and the nobility. The most effective device appeared to be ennoblement, a goal that Franz Joseph frequently satisfied, for the good reason, among others, that ennoblement taxes generated considerable revenue for the crown. However, the social access promised by titles proved elusive, a predicament expressed in the saying: "I beg your pardon, I am not from the Freyung!" (Ich bitt'um Verzeihung, ich bin nicht von der Freyung!) The phrase, which refers to a small square in the "noble quarter" near the Hofburg, caricatured the situation of the new aristocracy, which vainly strove to be assimilated into the old. The servile excess with which the "Ring Barons" imitated their chosen models and their conspicuous flaunting of new wealth did little but provoke dismissal as "shop-window displays." Such vulgar compensation for an inferiority complex proved hopeless as a method for bridging the social gap.

With the development of the fashionable Ring, Vienna experienced a boom in palais architecture second only to that of the Baroque age. The Ring, conceived from the start as the via triumphalis of the Habsburg dynasty, gained all-important social cachet from the presence there of mansions built by the Archdukes Wilhelm and Ludwig Viktor, as well as by such old aristocratic families as the Württembergs, Hoyos, and Kinskys. The distinguished Aristocrats' Casino also took a position on the Ringstrasse. Aesthetically, the Ring gave rise to a distinctive style and achieved it at the highest possible level of quality. The results, though admired by contemporaries, have enjoyed little recognition in subsequent times. It took a long while for eclectic historicism to be accepted as a legitimate style and acknowledged for its significance and beauty. Twentieth-century modernists have loathed it to the point of damnation, just as the Baroque had been a hundred years before.

This hostile judgment derived from the completely different, aggressively antihistorical taste of the new century, with its egalitarian values and "form follows function" and "less is more" aesthetics. The

The Schwarzenbergplatz with the Ring palais of Archduke Ludwig Viktor. Chromolithgoraph by Franz Alt.

The library in the Palais Dumba, c. 1887. Watercolor by Rudolf v. Alt.

view of historicism as the "styleless style" (stated by Egon Friedell in his History of Contemporary Art) naturally exacted its toll. The Ring palais also suffered from the new, nonresidential uses to which they were put, with the consequence that the interiors of Ring mansions, once monuments to a specific way of life, have survived so little as to become a great rarity.

The keynote of the Ring style is an architectural vocabulary drawn from all historical periods combined with the exploitation of modern materials and technology. The style was meant to satisfy contemporary needs and demands while preserving the symbolic value of older forms. Gothic proved irresistible for major religious and municipal structures, while the Renaissance and Roman Baroque found favor in private palais. During the half-century of the Ring period, the outward appearance of the palais built along the great circular boulevard changed considerably. In historicism's early romantic phase, smooth, serene faìades with small-scale, delicately wrought embellishments dominated. In its Classical phase, historicism produced more dramatically articulated faìades – more varied, dynamic, and three-dimensional. Finally, the style culminated in a bewildering profusion, where even Secessionist (modernist or Art Nouveau) elements began to appear.

The Baroque palais, in its more ostentatious aspects, yielded the principal model for the Ring palais, the splendor of whose portal, vestibule, and staircase competed with the 17th-18th-century prototype. But the centerpiece of the Ring palais was the salon, its social significance clearly evident in the importance accorded the piano nobile – the main upstairs floor – in the composition of the façade. Indeed, the salon became the focus of the search for the Gesamtkunstwerk, the total work of art in which all the arts played

roles of equal importance. Coffered ceilings with inset paintings, huge chandeliers and candelabras, carved paneling, sumptuous curtains and valences counted as heavily in the overall lavish effect as the arrangement of the seating furniture. Completing the ensemble were the palms and massive bouquets popularized by the painter Hans Makart, richly colored and patterned carpets, and whole congeries of treasures assembled from every conceivable age and culture.

The leading historicist architects included Gottfried Semper, Karl von Hasenauer, August Sicard von Sicardsburg, Eduard van der Nüll, Theophil von Hansen, and Heinrich von Ferstel, all of them occupied primarily with the design of the monumental public buildings that rose along the Ring. Only Hansen and Ferstel executed commissions for major private palais. Among the busiest designers of Ring mansions figured August Schwendenwein Ritter von Lonauberg and Johann Romano Ritter vom Ringe, the particle in the latter's name referring to his work on the Ring. However, the galvanizing personality of the period was the painter Hans Makart, the "divine magician" who set the tone for Ring society in both his lifestyle and in his painting.

The final phase in the construction of the Hofburg began under Emperor Franz Joseph. However, the plans drawn up by Semper and Hasenauer for a monumental Imperial forum on the Ring would be realized only in part. Still, considering the quality of the Neue Burgand the two Court Museums, the 19th-century Hofburg emerges as a powerful work. The fact that it survives as a mere fragment – a torso without limbs – yields the advantage of allowing us to read the entire history of how the great complex came into being, a vast palace to which every style of architecture made its contribution.

Today, the Hofburg stands as a multiform complex whose history stretches over more than six centuries. Just as the Imperial residence developed from fortress into palace, so did Vienna evolve from a cramped, walled-in burgher town to a great metropolis of opulent palais. The Viennese palais give visible testimony to that grand and eventful history. In their individuality and variety they have set their mark on the face of the Austrian capital, which, thanks in no small part to its aristocratic residences, lives on as one of the finest cities in the world.

Town Palais

The Hofburg

The Hofburg – also known as the "Winter Palace" – was begun in 1275, according to the contemporary chronicles written by the Bohemian King Ottokar II, sovereign of Austria, who built a castle within the circuit of defense walls surrounding Vienna, near a gate called Widmertor.

Barely a year later, Ottokar found himself forced to surrender both castle and town to Germany's King Rudolf of Habsburg (r. 1273-91). With this, Rudolf founded the long-lived Habsburg dynasty of Austria, whose monarchs would forever retain the castle as their winter residence. The oldest part of today's Hofburg – a quadrangular section surrounding the so-called Schweizerhof – dates all the way back to Ottokar's time. However, the name "Swiss Court" is fairly recent, stemming as it does from the Swiss guard in the service of Emperor Franz I Stephan von Lothringen (Lorraine), the consort of Maria Theresia. Originally, the Hofburg constituted a purely defensive castle, fortified with four mighty corner towers and an encircling moat, which survives partly intact. Also still present from the medieval fortress is the chapel. First mentioned in 1296, this sanctuary underwent reconstruction and expansion in 1447-49, during the reign of Emperor Friedrich III. Today, it is largely obscured by other buildings, and only the Gothic chancel can be seen in the Kapellenhof.

When Ferdinand I (r. 1552-64) shifted his residence from Prague to Vienna, he had the castle enlarged to include lavishly furnished private

page 18: Heraldic frescoes on the vaults of the Schweizertor.
pages 18-19: View over the Volksgarten towards the Amalienburg, the Leopoldine Wing, and the dome of the Michaelerkuppel.

left: Gothic figures of saints in the Burgkapelle.

quarters and then restyled in the manner of the Italian Renaissance. This campaign of construction yielded the magnificent Schweizertor, or "Swiss Gate," completed in 1552-53. Then came Stallburg Castle, which Ferdinand had erected for his son Archduke Maximilian following the latter's return from Spain. The outer façade is largely devoid of articulation, but the courtyard within is completely surrounded by handsome, open arcades on all three floors. When Maximilian ascended the throne in 1564, he had the court stables moved here. Eventually, the Stallburg would also house the royal art collections. Today, it is home to the Spanish Riding School, as well as to the Court Apothecary Shop, which dates back to 1745.

The Amalienburg, commissioned by Emperor Rudolf II in 1575, stands between the Inner Courtyard and a square known as the Ballhausplatz. It was designed by Pietro Ferrabosco, who in 1581 also took charge of the building's construction, producing another quadrangular edifice, this one wrapped about a trapezoidal courtyard. In the second half of the 17th century, the building gained its top floor as well as the present clock tower. The Amalienburg was named for Josef I's Empress, who spent her widowhood here. During the Congress of Vienna (1814-15), Tsar Alexander I took up residence

in a suite of rooms in the Amalienburg. Later in the 19th century, Empress Elisabeth, the wife of Emperor Franz Josef, would live in another section of the same palace.

Leopold I (r. 1658-1705), the first "Baroque Emperor," decided to expand the Hofburg on a grandiose scale, a project that went forward in the years 1660-66. Inspired by the Residenz in Munich, Leopold had a splendid building constructed that would provide a link between the old castle and the Amalienburg. This accounts for the unusual length of the Leopoldine Wing that Philibert Lucchese designed, a structure that succumbed to fire only a short time after its completion. It was then rebuilt by Pietro Tencala, who created the present façade. Maria Theresia as well as her son and successor, Josef II, occupied suites in this wing. Today, it constitutes the luxurious seat of the President of the Austrian Federation.

The most magnificent part of the Baroque Hofburg is the Hofbibliothek, or Court Library, commissioned by Karl VI in 1721. Johann Bernhard Fischer von Erlach designed the project, and his son Emanuel oversaw its construction. The exterior was completed in 1726 and the rest of the building in 1735. The Court Library represents Viennese Baroque architecture at its most evolved, and it survives as the crowning achievement of Fischer von Erlach, being both his last and most glorious work. Dominating the main façade is a tall, almost freestanding entrance pavilion coiffed by a magnificent imperial dome. The interior, meanwhile, is altogether as monumental as the exterior.

In 1763, Nikolaus Pacassi undertook to shore up the Court Library, a procedure made necessary by the settling of the foundation. At the same time, he altered both the façades and the height of the two

*The Schweizertor over
the old moat.*

*The arcaded courtyard of the
Stallburg.*

The statue of Francis II in the Inner Courtyard, with the Amalienburg in the background (left) and the Leopoldine Wing (below).

adjoining buildings to make them more complementary to Fischer von Erlach's architecture. The result is the harmonious, U-shaped ensemble known as the Josefsplatz.

Johann Lukas von Hildebrandt received the commission to build the Reichkskanzleitraktes, or Imperial Chancellery, which would culminate in the Burgplatz. On the northeast side of the Hofburg complex, the Chancellery would house the most important of all the government offices, the Aulic Council. Three years later, Josef Emanuel Fischer von Erlach became responsible for continuing work on and adding to the Chancellery, designing as well the long, handsome main façade, with its colossal pilasters and its balconies overhanging the entrance portals. Sculptural accents are provided not only by Lorenzo Mattielli's Herculean reliefs on either side of the entrance doors, but also by massive crowns placed like keystones atop rounded-headed arches and the freestanding attic figures posed upon the cornice. It was in the Aulic Council that Franz Josef established his reception and living chambers, most of which are now open to the public.

Emperor Karl VI commissioned the third section of the Baroque Hofburg – the Winter Riding School – which Fischer von Erlach built in the years 1729-35 on the site of the former "Paradise Garden." To the world at large, the huge riding hall with its colonnaded galleries constitutes the most famous part within the entire Hofburg complex, thanks to the regular performances given there by the beautiful white Lippizaner horses of the Spanish Riding School. Fischer von Erlach also planned the wing known as Michaelertrakt, designed to link the Winter Riding School with the Aulic Council. However, it was not until 1889-93 that Burghauptmann Ferdinand Kirschner brought the Michaelertrakt to completion in a neo-Baroque style.

Under Emperor Franz II (the last Emperor of the Holy Roman Empire [r. 1792-1806], who, beginning in 1804, would reign, until 1835, as Emperor Franz I of Austria), the great Ceremonial Hall came into being in 1802-06, conceived in the Classical manner by the architect Louis von Montoyer and situated at right angles to the new building at the southeast end of the Leopoldine Wing.

When the French withdrew their forces and ended their occupation of Vienna in 1809, Napoleon had the Hofburg's fortifications blown up. This cleared the way for the Volksgarten and Kaisergarten

24

(today the Burggarten), between which Pietro Nobile inserted the Outer Burg Square and its gate.

Once the encircling defense walls of old Vienna had been removed, the Hofburg gained its broad, hemicyclical Imperial Forum at the same time that the Ringstrasse was underway. Started in 1881, construction on the Neuen or "New" Burg ended only in 1913, on a vast but nonetheless reduced scale relative to the ambitious scheme drawn up by Gottfried Semper and Karl von Hasenauer. Even though dogged by financial as well as aesthetic problems, the Imperial Forum emerged as an extremely impressive structure, one that carried the monumentalism of the so-called "Ringstrasse Epoch" to its climax.

The Hofburg, whose history stretches all the way from the 13th century to the beginning of the 20th, looms large among the most important showplaces in Europe. The extraordinary record of its role as the residence of rulers, Kings, and Emperors can be found in the Sacred and Secular Treasuries in the Schweizertrakt. In addition to its Court Library, museums, and many other institutions, the Hofburg today houses an international conference center, where the future organization of a united Europe is debated.

page 24: The façade of the Court Library on Josefsplatz (above) and the Aulic Council Wing on the Burgplatz (below).
page 25: The office of the Austrian Federal President, formerly a room in the private apartments of Emperor Josef II. The painting portrays four daughters of the Empress Maria Theresia performing an opera.

opposite: The "Pietra-dura Room,"
in Maria Theresia's suite in the
Leopoldine Wing, contains the
world's largest collection of paintings
executed in pietra-dura, a stone
marquetry technique developed in
Florence during the 18th century.

Behind the monuments to Archduke
Karl and Prince Eugene of Savoy,
which inspired the name
Heldenplatz or "Heroes' Square,"
the crescent-shaped façade of the
"New" Burg sweeps across the
background.

27

The Archbishop's Palace

In the second half of the 13th century, the St. Stephen's parish quadrangle occupied the site of today's Archepiscopal Palace, which lies between Stephansplatz, Rotenturmstrasse, and Wollzeile. With the erection of St. Stephen's Church, the old residence came to be known as a Propsthof,

or "provost's quandrangle," and then Bishofshof as the parish grew into a bishopric. In 1627, a fire totally destroyed the building.

By 1723, the dwelling had assumed the importance of Archbishop's Palace, the actual structure commissioned by Bishops Anton Wolfrath and Friedrich Philipp Count Breuner and erected in 1632-41 from designs by Giovanni Coccapani. It was given a simple, Early Baroque façade. Simultaneously, the original Gothic chapel – whose apse now projects into Stephansplatz – was renovated, a process that included embellishing the structure with Early Baroque features and elaborating the interior with lavish stucco work. Dedicated to St. Andrew, the chapel contains altars from Vienna's Augustinian Church and the Church of St. Peter. The courtyard, with its partially blind arcades, is divided in two by the library wing. On the west side stands a monumental wall fountain with statues.

After 1716, Bishop (later Prince-Archbishop) Siegmund Count Kollonitsch had the façade enriched with additional stucco work, including the shell motifs over the windows that give the main building its present appearance. The arms of the Kollonitsch family, together with the Archbishop's hat, can be seen above the portal.

left: The voluted arms of the Kollonitsch family and a bishop's hat adorn the main portal to the Archepiscopal Palace.

below: One of the Heidentürme, or "Heathens' Towers," of St. Stephen's Cathedral rises above the arcaded courtyard of the Archbishop's Palace.

The choir of the old Gothic
chapel projects from the
Archbishop's Palace into
Stephansplatz.

opposite: The Pauper's Altar in the Andreaskapelle, or St. Andrew's Chapel, once stood in the Augustinian Church.

The staircase (right) and library (below) in the Archbishop's Palace.

Palais Starhemberg

This palais gained its present form – a freestanding, quadrangular building erected about an inner courtyard – only in 1895, when, following demolition of the house next door, the great mansion was extended westward by three bays, to make a total of thirteen sets of windows facing Minoritenplatz. With this, the entrance portal ceased to be asymmetrically placed and fell exactly at the center of the new façade, which was styled in full consistency with the old architecture.

The small palais the enlarged Stahremberg displaced was already there in 1661 when Konrad Balthasar Count Starhemberg acquired his property and had it cleared for fresh building. As completed, this structure is known from a depiction dated 1687. In 1683, the year of the second, critical siege, the palais was owned by the builder's son, Ernest Rüdiger Count Starhemberg, who happened also to be the military governor of Vienna and thus an architect of the Austrian defense against the Turks.

The Starhemberg Palais ranks with the Leopoldine Wing of the Hofburg as one of the best-preserved Early Baroque structures in Vienna. Although a bit four-square and flat, the monumental façade is saved from utter monotony by the relief effects of the heavy, sculpturesque pediments above the windows of the two principal stories. At the level of the top mezzanine, the pilasters between the bays are decorated with putti serving as caryatids for the massive consoles that support the overhanging roof.

While the façade has remained largely intact, the interior underwent thorough renovation in 1784. Based on designs by the architect Andreas Zach, the alterations affected mainly the state apartments, the entrance, and the staircase, which was now ornamented with figures by Josef Kleiber. The conference chamber, with its elegant ensemble of white and gold, constitutes an important example of interior décor from the reign of Josef II (1765-90). The uncommonly rich stucco work on the ceilings in the Ministerzimmers, or "Ministerial Rooms," and other salons has no parallel elsewhere in Vienna. After many changes of ownership, the Palais Starhemberg was acquired by the state in 1871 for the Ministry of Religion and Education, which brought about the enlargement cited above. Today, the palace houses the ministries for education, the arts, and sports, as well as those for science and research.

A richly stuccoed and painted ceiling.

One of the Ministerial Rooms, this one superbly decorated in the Empire manner.

*The Palais Starhemberg
viewed in all its massiveness
from Minoritenplatz.*

35

Palais Lobkowicz

In 1685-87, shortly after the great victory over the Turks outside Vienna, Philipp Sigmund Count Dietrichstein had a palais erected in the old Schweinemarkt ("Pig Market") on the site of the Fellschen House and the Dorotheer Baths. Today, the structure bears the name of a later owner, Prince von Lobkowicz. After soliciting ideas from Peter Strudel, Giovanni Pietro Tencala, and a third, unknown architect, Count Dietrichstein adopted the proposal submitted by Tencala. But as early as 1710, the long, extended façade was altered by Johann

Bernard Fischer von Erlach, who followed the trend towards emphatic symmetry and centrality. In its original form, the street front had been articulated mainly by small-scale but strongly relieved features, as in the crisp definition of the pediments and the opulently turned consoles. Now, Fischer von Erlach capped the central bays with an attic and balustrade, the latter supporting a phalanx of freestanding statues, and then pierced the façade below with a new entrance portal. Here, the door is flanked by clusters of diagonally angled pilasters and Tuscan columns that culminate in urns with serpent volutes. The space between the latter is spanned by a balustraded balcony supported upon a tiara-like entablature sprung from the lower pilasters within the cluster on either side. Later, Emanuel Fischer von Erlach added the elaborately sculptural cartouche over the broad window above the door, where the Lobkowicz arms and coronet are borne aloft by figures on either side.

The barrel-vaulted entrance hall is flanked by side niches and focused upon a wall fountain reigned over by Hercules Triumphant. The staircase, supported by Tuscan columns and a barrel vault embellished with fine, low-relief stucco work, leads to the state rooms on the piano nobile. In the great ballroom the court painter Jacob von Schuppen decorated the ceiling with a splendid fresco allegorizing the arts. The enframing trompe-l'oeil architecture was executed by Marcantonio Chiarini.

In 1753, Wenzel Eusebius Prince von Lobkowicz acquired the palais, where, in 1804, Beethoven's Eroica Symphony would receive its first performance, under the baton of the composer himself, at a private function in the ballroom. Disappointed by Napoleon, Beethoven switched the dedication of his "heroic" score to his own generous patron, Franz Joseph Prince von Lobkowicz. During the Congress of Vienna, the Palais Lobkowicz became a favorite gathering place and the scene of many splendid balls. Since 1991, the restored mansion has been the home of the Austrian Theater Museum.

page 39: The frescoed ceiling of the ballroom of the Palais Lobkowicz.

page 40: A detail of the frescoed ceiling in the ballroom and a view of the grand staircase.
page 41: The Hercules grotto fountain in the entrance hall.

The main façade with its entrance portal altered by Johann Bernard Fischer von Erlach.

41

Palais Liechtenstein

With the pronounced classicism of its faìade, which runs along the Bankgasse (formerly Vordere Schenkenstrasse), the Palais Liechtenstein reflects the Roman Baroque in all its formal qualities. The quadrangul ar, four-storied mass of the building rises about an inner

courtyard behind a main front articulated by a lightly projected central section. Embellished with columns and figural sculptures, the great portal opens into an entrance hall five bays wide. Apart from the series of mighty pilasters marking off its central section, the façade confronts the world in a calm, clear, almost flat manner, with the result that, like its great Italian prototypes, the Palais Liechtenstein radiates dignity and grandezza. Still, it speaks with an Austrian accent, thanks to the main portal and, especially, to the beautiful side portal on the Minoritenplatz, as well as to the statues above the attic.

In 1691 or 1692, the master mason Antonio Riva began constructing the palace from plans drawn up by Domenico Martinelli. His client, Count Dominik Andreas Kaunitz, had acquired the land from the Khe venhıller family, who had been planning to build a palais of their own on what is a choice site within the noble quarter. On 23 April 1694, the structure, which had not risen above the ground floor, found itself with a new owner, Prince Hans Adam von Liechtenstein, who reassigned the project to Gabriele di Gabrieli. By 1705 the palace was completed, albeit with some arbitrary alter-ations, most notably in the form of the staircase.

A number of important Italian artists collaborated in creating the building's décor, among them Giovanni Giuliani who contributed the sumptuous statuary, Santino Bussi the stucco work, and Andrea L nzani the frescoed ceilings, which have not survived.

During the years 1836-47 Prince Alois von Liechtenstein made a number of drastic modifications on the interior, carried out by Peter Hubert Devigny, who refurbished the great ballroom in the "Second Rococo" style, which superseded Biedermeier. Indeed, the rooms redone in the neo-Rococo manner at the Palais Liechtenstein are the most important of their kind in Vienna.

Because of its magnificent interior and the splendid art collections it contained, the Palais Liechtenstein became a legendary house. But it also earned renown for the technical features incorporate d during the renovation, features that allowed the size and height of the rooms to be changed. However, they were also very much subject to breakdown and thus in need of constant maintenance and freq uent repair, which made the palace known as the "artists' workshop." Yet when functional, the "lifting machines" and the movable walls and ceilings were sensational novelties that never failed to ast onish visitors. The devices reflected the openness of the Prince to technology and its revolutionary innovations.

The great and universally admired rooms suffered grave damage in 1945, during the final days of World War II. Also affected was the opulently decorated staircase, which, however, would be fully rest ored by 1976. The palace is still the Viennese residence of the reigning Prince of Liechtenstein.

The main portal on Bankgasse (below) and the side entrance on Minoritenplatz (opposite).

44

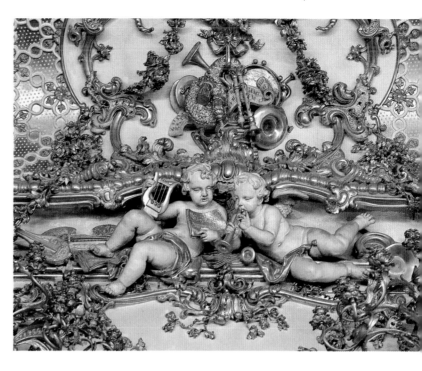

pages 46/47: The stylistically varied salons at the Palais Liechtenstein form a suite evincing the highest aesthetic refinement.

The magnificent staircase animated by the playful statuary of Giovanni Giuliani. whole of his fortune to the poor of Vienna.

Palais Harrach

In its many depictions, the Freyung is usually dominated by the Palais Harrach. Indeed, the square has long been associated with the Harrach family. As early as 1600, a house on this spot was owned by Baron (later Count) Karl von Harrach, the father-in-law of Albrecht von Wallenstein (or Waldstein) – Austria's famous General during the Thirty Years War – who stayed there many times. After the Auerspergs received the house as a gift, it caught fire and burned during the Turkish siege of 1683. Count Ferdinand Bonaventure von Harrach bought back the charred ruin and, after 1690, had Domenico Martinelli come specially from Rome to replace it with a new palais. Nevertheless, the house was once misattributed to the Harrachs' "house architect," Johann Lukas von Hildebrandt, who had merely created the "Salettl," a pavilion that used to stand in the little garden on the unbuilt corner between the Freyung and Herrengasse – one of the extremely rare palais gardens within the inner city. The Salettl underwent radical alteration in the mid-19th century, and then disappeared altogether during World War II, when the palais itself suffered considerable damage.

While the façade along Herrengasse retains the essentials of its Early Baroque form, the main façade on the Freyung and the interior have been greatly modified. The small chapel, with its ceiling attributed to the painter Johann Michael Rottmayr, is well preserved. Until 1970, Palais Harrach housed one of Vienna's most important private collections of paintings, which, following a division of property, is now in Schloss Rohrau, the family castle in Lower Austria. The collection came into being as a direct result of the Harrachs' various diplomatic activities. Ferdinand Bonaventura, as Ambassador from the Holy Roman Empire to Spain and France, acquired numerous pictures by Spanish and French masters, after which his son Alois Thomas, while serving as Viceroy of Naples, enriched the Viennese collection with Neapolitan works. Then, Alois' son collected Flemish and Dutch masters during his tenure as Obersthofmeister at the court of the Stadtholder of the Netherlands.

Another Count Harrach, Karl Borromäus, was well known in Vienna for his humanitarian interests. As a doctor, he devoted his life to caring for the poor. He also maintained relations with Goethe and other poets as well as scholars. In 1814, Count Karl Borromäus became primarius at the Elisabeth Hospital in Landstrasse. He died in 18??, leaving the whole of his fortune to the poor of Vienna.

The stuccoed ceiling in the entrance hall, surmounted by the staircase balustrade.

In the staircase, a marble-framed door crowned by the Harrach arms.

opposite: The Freyung with the Palais Harrach, engraving by J.A. Delsenbach after J.E. Fischer von Erlach.

A Baroque ceiling at the Palais Harrach depicting a mythological scene.

The chapel in the Palais Harrach dedicated to the Immaculate Conception.

53

Palais Mollard-Clary

Peter von Mollard, who was Imperial Chamberlain and Master of the Emperor's Horse, acquired the house on Herrengasse in the second half of the 16th century. His five sons played important political roles, especially Ernst, who figured prominently at the court of Rudolf II and served as Governor of Lower Austria. For a long while there stood "a Mollard behind every Habsburg." Yet, despite their successful careers, which brought them substantial gifts as well as elevation to the rank of Count, the Mollards never ceased to have financial difficulties. Even the rebuilding of the palais in the 1690s obliged Ferdinand Ernst Count von Mollard to apply for a loan. Domenico Martinelli drew up the plans, perhaps in collaboration with Domenico Egidio Rossi. The client rejected the simple design prepared by Martinelli for the façade and portico, but accepted his proposal for the interior. The capable Tyrolean builder Christian Alexander Oedtl assumed the task of building the palais. Meanwhile, Ferdinand's sister, Countess Fuchs, won fame as "Fuchsin," the nurse, Chief Stewardess, and confidante of Maria Theresia, as well as the only non-Habsburg ever to be buried in the Imperial family's Capuchin vault.

On 29 September 1760 the Mollards sold the palais to Counts Wenzel von Clary und Aldringen, in whose family it would remain until 1922. The Clarys enjoyed a great reputation less for their political activities than for their noble, aesthetic high-mindedness. For several years around 1780, the Palais Mollard-Clary was the regular scene of Josef II's "round table," a circle that included the Emperor, Prince Orsini-Rosenberg, General Franz von Lacy, and "five Princesses": Maria Leopoldine Kaunitz, Josefa Clary, Sidonie Kinski, Eleonore Liechtenstein, and Maria Leopoldine Liechtenstein.

The Clarys had the palais' façade rebuilt towards the end of the 18th century, a campaign that produced the two tower-like corners and the colossal pilasters that define the central bays in between. It was also now that the elaborately gilded decorative grilles under the main-floor windows were brought from the family's estate at Teplice in Bohemia. The engaged columns of rusticated stone blocks on either side of the entrance portal support an elegantly curved and balustraded balcony, under which the allegorical figures of Wisdom and Vigilance fill the spandrels of the arch. Although the interior has undergone numerous alterations according to the taste of the day, the picturesque décor in the gallery on the piano nobile survives from the turn of the 18th century. Here, oil paintings executed directly upon plaster depict mytholgoical scenes populated by groups of putti, which may be the work of the Milanese painter Andrea Lanzani.

After 1831, the British Embassy found a home on the third floor of the Palais Mollard-Clary. In his memoirs entitled A Victorian in Vienna, Ambassador Sir Horace Rumpold provides a fascinating insight into the social life of Vienna during the late Biedermeier period.

Since 1924 the palais has housed the Museum of Lower Austria.

left and above: The gallery, with oil paintings on a gold ground.

overleaf: The façade of the Palais Mollard-Clary with its original entrance portal.

opposite: Roggendorfer Altar, c. 1500. Collection of the Museum of Lower Austria housed in the Palais Mollard-Clary.

Palais Esterházy

According to an inscription on a plaque in the courtyard, this palais was "acquired through His Highness Paul Esterházy, Prince of the Holy Roman Empire, Palatine of the Kingdom of Hungary, and to the glory of the family who built [the palais] from the ground up in its present form." Previously, the site had been occupied by several burgher houses. With its unifying series of colossal pilasters, the well-balanced façade leaves no doubt about its source hn Italian Baroque architecture, despite the effects of various subsequent alterations. The architect is thought to have been a member of the circle around Giovanni Pietro Tencala. The great depth of today's Palais Esterházy results from later additions made on the side facing Naglergasse.

The focal point of the façade is the large portal at the center, with its overhead balcony carried on sumptuously carved consoles and its wrought-iron grille displaying the Esterházys' gilded arms. An armorial cartouche also blazes forth from the pediment over the window giving onto the balcony. A tower in the courtyard signals the existence of a chapel within, a structure with Baroque features dedicated in 1699 to St. Leopold by Cardinal Leopold Count Kolonitsch. In the mid-18th century the larger salons received a décor of chinoiseries and delicate stucco work. Another room was later renovated in a splendid Empire style.

Franz Joseph Haydn, as director of the Esterházy orchestra, conducted regularly in the palais in Wallnerstrasse. It was here, in the presence of Admiral Nelson and Lady Hamilton, that he gave the first performance of his Lord Nelson Mass.

below: A painting of St. Leopold from the Baroque period hangs above the altar in the palais chapel.

opposite: The Empire room in the Palais Esterházy dates from the early 19th century.

right: The main façade of the Palais Esterházy in Wallnerstrasse.

below: The inscription over an arched passage in the courtyard cites 1695 as the year of the palais' construction.

The Winter Palais
of Prince Eugene

Barely ten years after he joined the Imperial Army in 1683, Prince Eugene of Savoy had advanced to the rank of Field Marshal and become a public figure of great fame, power, and wealth. He then redirected his energies towards the construction of a magnificent town palais, beginning with the purchase of a burgher house in the street known as Himmelpfortgasse. Along with this property, he also bought the garden of Count Karl Maximilian von Thun and the barns of the Herbersteins adjoining it. His plans, moreover, included the possibility of later acquiring other houses adjacent to his core holdings. To design the palais, Prince Eugene engaged Johann Bernhard Fischer von Erlach, who worked on the project from 1695 to 1698, doing so in a manner that would permit the seven-bay mansion to be subsequently enlarged, as the client purchased more land, and yet remain a harmonious whole.

In Fischer von Erlach, a self-confident, aesthetically sophisticated client found the ideal collaborator, one who understood how to make the new palais express not only the owner's military and political success but also his erudition, taste, and love of art. Thus, it is the heroic Hercules and Apollo, the god of the muses, who dominate the iconographical program on both the inside and the outside of Prince Eugene's Winter Palais.

The façade generally reflects the conventions of the Early Baroque, albeit combined with the form language of High Baroque. Articulated by a continuous row of colossal pilasters, the long façade – twice extended to a total of ten additional bays – brought to something of a climax the overall unity, or even monotony, of Early Baroque palais architecture, with its endless unfolding of like elements. In keeping with this tendency, the portals scarcely project at all. Moreover, the sculpture on either side of the entrances is bas-relief, at least by comparison with the richer plasticity of the figural sculptures on the balconies and the convoluted pediments of the piano nobile. This main floor rests upon a base one and a half stories high, so that more light can pour into the state rooms, despite the darkening effect of a narrow street.

In 1702, Prince Eugene replaced Fischer von Erlach with Johann Lukas von Hildebrandt, whom the Prince had come to know from his work on fortifications during the Italian campaigns. For the enlargements that followed, Hildebrandt adhered to the original plans, just as his patron no doubt wished. In 1708-09, the architect completed the five-bay gallery wing on the east, and then, 1723-24, the five-bay library wing on the west, constructed after the neighboring house had been acquired in 1719. The result is the strictly symmetrical façade that we know today, stretching through seventeen bays and pierced by three portals, all of them alike.

The great reception rooms came into being with the original core structure built by Fischer von Erlach, as did also the grand ceremonial staircase. For the interior décor, Prince Eugene called upon the most famous artists of the day. Beginning with the richly stuccoed vestibule, a work by Santino Bussi, the courtly, aristocratic society of 18th-century Vienna found itself deeply impressed. Thereafter, the splendor became even more so as guests approached

the staircase and discovered the mighty Atlas caryatids, by Giovanni Giuliani; it culminated in the state or reception rooms of the piano nobile, all fitted out by a multitude of contemporary artists. Here, among the most important rooms, are the Gold Cabinet, with its sumptuously molded and gilded ceiling, and the Audience Chamber as well as the Parade Room (today known as the Red and Blue Salons). Some of the spaces would be altered in later years.

The decorative scheme was systematic and all-embracing, from the beautiful floors through the gilt woodwork ornamented with grotesques, to the exquisite fabrics hung on the walls and the frescoes painted on the ceilings. Then came the painted overdoors, the mirrors, and the oil paintings, the crystal chandeliers and sconces, the superb furniture. Johann Basilius Küchelbecker, writing in his Newest Information about the Holy Roman Imperial Court (1730), summed it up thus: "Nothing has been spared that could possibly enhance the splendor of this palace."

When Prince Eugene died in 1736 without direct heirs, his entire estate went to his niece, Victoria of Savoy, who, one by one, sold all the treasures that had been so lovingly assembled by the Prince. Emperor Karl VI acquired the famous library and etching collection for his recently established Court Library. The art works were scattered. Maria Theresia bought the palais in 1752 to house the Coin and Mining Office. In 1798, the central finance office – called the "Imperial and Imperial-Royal Court

The famous ceremonial staircase in Prince Eugene's Winter Palais.

Chamber for Finance and Commerce – moved in. Today, the Winter Palais of Prince Eugene is the headquarters of the Federal Ministry for Finance.

below: The Gold Cabinet, a prime example of Baroque exuberance.

Palais Caprara

This palais rose on Wallnerstrasse during the last years of the 17th century, at the behest of Field Marshal Enea Silvio Count of Caprara, who was a nephew of Ottavio Piccolomini and a cousin of Count Montecuccoli. Much uncertainty and considerable divergence of opinion surrounded both the date and the authorship of this building until research, by Günther Passavent and Wilhelm Georg Rizzi, produced persuasive new evidence, which coincided with that yielded by a complete renovation of the building in 1986-88. The main creative force behind the structure is now known to have been the Bolognese painter and architect Domenico Egidio Rossi, who was active in Vienna and Bohemia in the 1690s. Very likely, Domenico Martinelli and Antonio Beduzzi were also involved in the planning and design of the Palais Caprara.

As a somewhat odd presence within the context of Vienna, the Palais Caprara has always drawn attention. Albert Ilg objected to the "altogether bizarre style of this arresting and monumental building, which is out of keeping with Vienna's general appearance in the Baroque period." The Viennese chronicler Hermine Cloeter also concluded about the Palais Caprara: "There is something almost massive and heavy about it, as though it were not fluent in the language and gestures of the Viennese Baroque, had not, so to speak, quite discovered its own personal note, its peculiar charm and verve: in short, the building bears an alien feature on its face. . . ." Obviously, the unusual and striking aspects of the mansion emerged from the rank and origin of the owner. The descendant of an old Bolognese family, a member of the Imperial Council of War, and a Knight of the Golden Fleece, Caprara must have introduced the "alien" elements as a deliberate, even provocative way to parade his Italian origins and proclaim his elevated status, which he may have thought all the more necessary because of the palais' location somewhat at the edge of the noble quarter. The façade in particular would appear to reflect all these various issues and ambitions.

The style of the façade, with its five-bay central section flanked by pairs of projecting bays, its dramatically articulated division between stories, and the relatively high relief of all its elements, derives from the palazzo architecture of Northern Italy – especially Bologna. The mighty entrance portal framed by atlantes supporting an ovoid balcony gives the central façade its focal point. Equally marked are the alternating round-headed and triangular pediments over the windows of the piano nobile. By comparison with the façade on the street, those within the courtyard are much less pronounced in their relief.

The vestibule, which runs athwart the entryway, is an uncommonly spacious colonnade, from which the staircase leads to the piano nobile. Until divided up, the great hall occupied the full length of its wing and was entirely decorated with architectural paintings. The fragments discovered in the course of the latest restoration disclose a kind of trompe-l'oeil painting that was rare in Vienna's High Baroque.

In April 1786, the Palais Caprara was sold to Prince Carl von Liechtenstein and a year after that to Baron Wimmer. In 1798, it was rented by the French Ambassador, Jean Baptiste Bernadotte, who later became King of Sweden. During a public celebration on 13 April, Bernadotte raised the tricolor of Revolutionary France, thereby setting off a storm with serious consequences. The infuriated populace

right: The main portal flanked by atlantes supporting a balcony.
below: The colonnaded vestibule in all its Italian charm.

tore the flag from the balcony and burned it in Am Hof Square. Bernadotte had to leave Vienna the next day.

In December 1798, the brothers Johann Heinrich and Johann Jakob Geymüller bought the palais for 135,525 gulden. The wealthy, artistically inclined Geymüllers had the interior redecorated according to contemporary taste and made the mansion a center of culture and society. It was at a musical soirée at the Geymüllers' Palais Caprara during the winter of 1820-21 that Franz Grillparzer met his "eternally beloved" Kathi Fröhlich. Two rooms from this period, complete with their exceptionally handsome Empire appointments, have been preserved: a salon, called the Geymüller Room, which remains in situ; and the so-called "Pompeian Room," now reinstalled, at full scale, in the Historical Museum of the City of Vienna. After many changes of ownership, the Palais Caprara became the home of the Museum of Lower Austria, but more recently it has been reborn as an office building.

opposite: The Geymüller Room is characteristic of the taste of Vienna's high bourgeoisie during the Biedermeier period.

72

Palais Batthyány-Schönborn

In 1698, Field Marshal Adam Count Batthyány acquired a house in Renngasse from Count Johann Weickhard von Sinzendorf and commissioned Johann Bernhard Fischer von Erlach to erect a new building in its place. The project must have been completed very quickly, for an engraving by Delsenbach from the year 1700

shows the main façade already in a finished state. The caption runs: "Façade of the building which his Excellency Adam von Batthyan, member of His Imperial and Royal Majesty's Privy Council and Ban of Croatia, had erected near Schottenplatz. Anno 1700."

The Palais Batthyány-Schönborn is one of the most distinctive works in Fischer von Erlach's oeuvre and in Viennese palais architecture generally, thanks mainly to the unusual design of the main façade. While the side sections have merely been rusticated in a light, delicate manner, the five central bays are quite richly decorated. And they would be even more so had they not lost their roof balustrade and the line of statues that once stood upon it, the absence of which deprives the façade of its important upward thrust. The decorative capitals of the tapered pilasters are works of high imagination. On either side of the engaged columns flanking the large portal are two pedestrian doors crowned by large urns set within upright oval niches. The beautifully worked reliefs over the windows of the piano nobile feature the Labors of Hercules. The climax of the entire decorative program on the façade comes in the elaborately sculptural cartouche atop the central

window, its figures, coat of arms, and coronet serving to glorify the palais' self-confident owner.

Tuscan columns support the three bays of the entrance hall, where the motif of vases in oval niches is repeated. The sparingly decorated staircase radiates a cool and noble splendor.

In 1740, Eleonore Countess Batthyány, the widow of the builder, sold the palais to Friedrich Karl Count von Schönborn, Imperial Vice-Chancellor and Bishop of Würzburg and Bamberg, who had the interior redecorated. The anonymous Description of Vienna, published in 1826, cited the importance of the collection owned by Franz Philipp Count von Schönborn-Buchheim, especially the painting by Rembrandt entitled The Blinding of Samson.

The library contains 20,000 precious volumes, including a nearly complete collection of travel literature and a Biblia Sacra dating from 1342. The palais in Renngasse remains in the possession of the Schönborn family to this day.

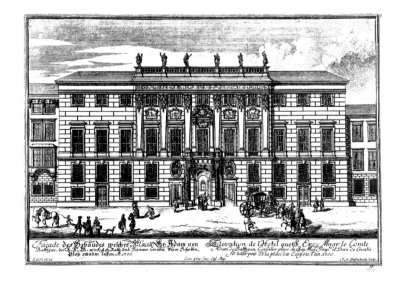

The rich variety of the central section
sets it apart from the rest of the
façade.

opposite: The palais façade,
engraving by J.A. Delsenbach after
J.E. Fischer von Erlach.

A view from the 1740 Red Salon
(below) into the statue-adorned
staircase (opposite).

Palais Daun-Kinsky

In Imperial times, the square known as Freyung was considered one of Vienna's most elegant and desirable addresses, a reputation it owed primarily to the presence there of not only the Palais Harrach but also the younger Palais Daun-Kinsky. The author of the latter mansion – an epitome of

aristocratic splendor – was Johann Lukas von Hildebrandt, who built it in the years 1713-16 for Count Wirich Philipp Lorenz von und zu Daun, Prince of Thiano, Privy Counselor and Treasurer, General Field Marshal, Commanding Officer of Vienna, later Viceroy of Naples-Sicily, Governor of the Austrian Netherlands, and Governor of Milan. The property itself left something to be desired, given that it consisted of a narrow strip of land lying perpendicular to the square and receding from it to a considerable depth. As a result, the usual six-bay structure, with its emphatic horizontality and social symbolism, could not be built. However, the problem merely inspired Hildebrandt to devise a brilliant solution, whereby the six-bay width would be translated into a six-story height, leaving the side wings to surround the inner courtyard instead of facing the square. And when it came to decorating the main façade, the staircase, and the great reception rooms, Hildebrandt simply transformed them into masterpieces. Altogether, the Palais Daun-Kinsky emerged as one of the architect's premier achievements, a festive world filled with Baroque fantasy and richness.

So crisp, clear, and shallow is the overall relief across the front that the façade gives the effect of paper-thin flatness. By tapering downwards, the giant pilasters that structure the central bays endow the façade with a soaring effect, even as their delicate arabesque traceries dangle in the opposite direction. The openwork balustrade along the attic, together with the statues and urns, adds to the overall sense of floating lightness. The large vertical entryway, which dominates the ensemble on the square, stands in marked contrast to the horizontal, diamond-shaped windows in the basement. Freestanding columns and atlantes flank the portal and support the powerful broken pediment above, where two allegorical figures recline while gesturing towards the princely builder's coat of arms, held aloft by putti.

A domed vestibule leads to the main staircase, which, with its lavish stucco work, counts among the most beautiful things of its kind in Vienna. The ceiling fresco, painted by Marcantonio Chiarini, presents a trompe-l'oeil scene of Imperial geniuses bearing a hero into the high heavens of warrior immortality. The allegorical ceiling frescoes in the oval great hall are by Carlo Carlone.

In 1746, Count Johann Joseph von Khevenhüller acquired the palais but then sold it in 1764 to Count Ferdinand Bonaventura von Harrach, whose daughter Rosa married Prince Kinsky. Thereafter the palais remained in the family's possession right up until 1986.

pages 80-81: The grand staircase, an
expression of the Baroque at its most
lavish.

opposite and below: The oval great
hall with ceiling frescoes by Carlo
Carlone.

The choir stalls in the dining room of the Palais Daun-Kinsky were built for the cathedral at Pressburg.

Palais Neupauer-Breuner

In 1715, Johann Christian Neupauer – town councillor, builder, and chamberlain – acquired three houses in Singerstrasse from the heirs of Count Karl Josef de Souches. On one of the sites he built a narrow, three-bay burgher house, while on the other two he erected his big town palais. By the mid-18th century, ruinous indebtedness caused the ownership of the palais to pass to the Suttner family, after which the mansion continued to change hands. Not until the end of the 19th century did the palais come to the Counts Breuner, through inheritance from the Duke of Ratibor and Corvey.

The façade of the building, whose architect remains unknown, consists of a mid-section with five sets of windows or bays and two wide wings each with three sets of windows. Despite the richness of the overall composition – especially the central section, a beautifully finished, well-integrated composition – the main portal makes itself felt as the real focal point. Here the big carriage entrance is flanked by two pedestrian doors, all structured by muscular atlantes supporting an entablature with balcony, urns, and sculptures of paired figures. The Breuner arms, held by putti, hang above the balcony door. From the three-bay entrance hall rises the staircase, which is uncharacteristically heated by a marble fireplace. This remarkable piece is decorated with a relief sculpture on a Herculean theme, carved by Matthäus Donner, the brother of the better-known Georg Raphael Donner. Marble statues and delicate stucco work complete the decorative scheme.

opposite: The exuberantly Baroque portal displays a wealth of sculptural invention.

below: The gallery of the Breuner family's ancestral portraits.

opposite: The marble fireplace in the stairwell of the Palais Neupauer-Breuner.

The salons of the piano nobile were redecorated in a contemporary style during the second half of the 19th century.

below: The palais façade and the Singerstrasse roofscape viewed from the Cathedral of St. Stephen.

Palais Fürstenberg

Two of the most striking features presented by the façade of this palais in Grünangergasse, built around 1720, are the diamond-faceted ashlar stones in the ground-floor masonry and the peculiar design of the entrance portal. From the strongly articulated base rises the smooth mass of the blocky building, whose featureless upper surfaces stand in marked contrast to the sculptural décor of the window frames. The architecture, like the navel spiral used as a decorative element, may recall Lukas von Hildebrandt, but the Palais Fürstenberg is more likely the work of the Bolognese artist Antonio Beduzzi.

The monumental entryway gives the main façade its chief point of interest. The naturalistically carved greyhounds, confronting one another from either side of the garland-draped arch, are most unusual. As heraldic creatures, they point to the builder, Imperial Councillor Johann Ernst Baron von Hatzenberg, whose palais the Fürstenberg Princes would not own until much later.

On the piano nobile the windows are decorated with enframing reliefs in the form of ribbon work and carved or modeled heads placed like keystones, themes that continue along the Domgasse façade. The richly stuccoed vestibule, where a bas-relief portrait of Josef II is mounted over the fireplace, leads to the staircase decorated with niched statues of Minerva, Mercury, Venus, and Hercules. Allegorical scenes in stucco work grace the ceiling of the ballroom, which was later converted into a library.

The entrance portal surmounted by rampant greyhounds.

*In the vestibule, a bas-relief portrait
of Josef II above the fireplace.*

*page 90: Niched statues of Venus and
Mercury in the staircase.
page 91: In the former ballroom, a
gloriously stuccoed Baroque ceiling.*

Palais Erdödy-Fürstenberg

I n 1720, Count Georg Erdödy had a palais built on Himmelpfortgasse to replace the house he had inherited in 1714. The architect of the new mansion is thought to have been the same as the anonymous author of the Palais Neupauer-Breuner, because of similarities in the form of their façades.

The parallels are especially notable in those parts that appear to have been inspired by Fischer von Erlach's Bohemian Chancellery. Again the portal is dramatized by means of mighty atlantes carrying a balcony with a balustrade of artfully pierced scrollwork. The unusual and marked verticality of the façade results from its relatively slender width, restricted to three central bays flanked by side wings of two bays each. Here, then, is a palais that recalls the tall, narrow, many-storied burgher house it replaced, leaving its palatial qualities to be centered upon the imposing character of the entrance portal. In 1825, Count Egon zu Fürstenberg had the interior redecorated.

The portal, with its powerful sculptures and decorations, is almost as imposing as a triumphal arch.

One of the portal's two atlantes.

The main façade of the Palais Erdödy-Fürstenberg, its tall, narrow form echoing the old burgher house it replaced.

Palais Rottal

Around 1750 the state acquired Count Rottal's palais, which had stood in Singerstrasse since the second half of the 17th century. It was then that Franz Hillebrand enlarged the building and brought the façade to its present form. Simultaneously, the mansion was combined with the building next door, which housed the Biliotte Foundation, established by Franz Biliotte, Emperor Leopold I's personal physician, to provide medical care for the poor of Vienna.

The old Palais Rottal was an elegant two-story building marked by a round tower on the corner of Grünangergasse. From this structure the vestibule remains, a three-bay, colonnaded hall that provides access to Hillebrand's splendid new staircase. The entrance portals also survive from the old mansion, complete with their strongly projecting broken pediments ridden by allegorical figures. They form part of a total three-bay composition that endows the otherwise monotonous façade with its principal interest. When a third story was added in 1842, the façade lost its crowning pair of triangular pediments to an attic designed in accordance with the old building and statues salvaged from the attic of Prince Eugene's Winter Palais.

The big Imperial arms on the attic recall the old, traditional way of identifying buildings as official. As for the Stadtbanco, or Town Bank, it became the home of the Ministry of Education in 1849, later housing the National Debt Office and other departments of the Ministry of Finance. Today, it accommodates the state's tax-inspection and legal-assistance services.

The strong relief of the twin portals enlivens the entire façade.

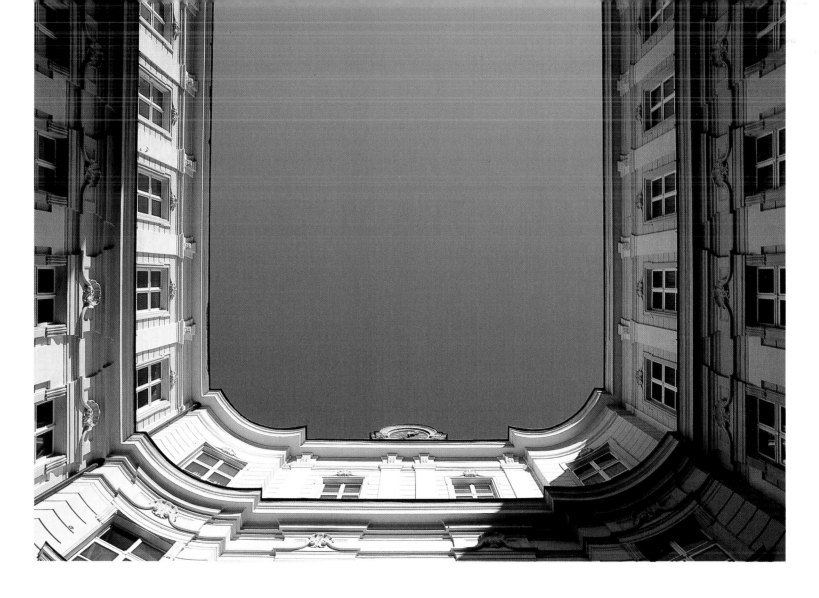

The elegant inner courtyard of the Palais Rottal.

page 98: The dome and a detail of the small chapel.
page 99: The salon decorated with gilded stucco work.

The compact vestibule, with its clusters of Tuscan columns, survives from the old aristocratic palais, while the grand staircase (opposite) was designed to serve the needs of an Imperial office.

Palais Dietrichstein

This double palais, charmingly situated on Minoritenplatz with a lateral façade on Metastasiogasse, comprises two older buildings. In 1755 Franz Hillebrand integrated them in such a manner as to achieve stylistic unity while also preserving most of their original elements. The result is a façade speaking the language of Late Baroque but with a fresh and delicate accent. For dramatic emphasis, the architect turned to the two entrance portals, where the beautiful Rococo door panels survive from the 18th century, as well as to the wide attic pediment with its figures of Chronos and Memoria reclining on either side of the triangle's apex.

In 1799, the Polish Chancellery moved into one of the mansions, while the other came into the possession of Maria Beatrix d'Este-Modena, the wife of Archduke Ferdinand, the fourth son of Maria Theresia. Following her death in 1806, the palais devolved upon the Princes Dietrichstein. Since 1955 it has belonged to the Austrian state.

Thanks to its rythmically alternated elements, the double façade resolves into a harmonious whole.

Palais Fries-Pallavicini

In this palais, built in 1783-84 on the Josefsplatz site of the old Queen's Convent, the architect Johann Ferdinand Hetzendorf von Hohenberg achieved the major secular work of his career. At its completion, however, the mansion created a tremendous scandal very similar so the one set off a century later by the Loos House on nearby Michaelerplatz. And the causes were similar, in that they had to do with styles that seemed too aggressively minimal for buildings as close as these to the Hofburg. So restrained are the compositional elements employed by Hetzendorf von Hohenberg that they

appeared devoid of the pomp expected of aristocratic dwellings. Instead, the structure radiates the nobility of cool equilibrium. Indeed, the only attention-getting features of the matter-of-fact block are the mezzanine floor – most unusual for Vienna – and the exceptionally tall windows immediately above on the piano nobile. Fierce polemics over the palais' radical simplicity forced the owner and his architect to compromise and give the façade some bit of grandeur. This came in the entrance portal, with its theatrically broken pediment and its flanking pairs of caryatids, furnished by the sculptor Franz Anton Zauner. However, the embellishment the same artist contributed to the attic had been planned from the start.

The enormously wealthy Johann (later Count) von Fries (1719-85), a banker, merchant, and industrialist from a respected family in Protestant Switzerland, gained his fortune in considerable part from the introduction of the Maria Theresia taler as a currency convertible for purposes of international trade. But while Johann Fries was a powerfully gifted and motivated man of affairs, his two sons, Joseph and Moritz, fell into the traditional category of the over-refined second generation, whose vast material advantages allowed them to live entirely for their personal interests, which in both cases happened to be the arts. Indeed, they became the Empire's most passionate collectors and patrons, with Joseph, the elder, achieving a pan-European reputation as such by the age of twenty. During his stay in Rome, Joseph frequented Goethe, as well as the painter Angelika Kauffmann, who did his portrait. The Palais Fries housed no fewer than 300 paintings, 400,000 engravings, and a library of some 16,000 precious volumes. The Frieses also owned a fabled collection of sculpture. Ludvig van Beethoven dedicated the Seventh Symphony to Moritz von Fries, his patron. As this would suggest, the Palais Fries was famous for the concerts and soirées held there. Karl Count Zinzendorf reports on one event, which occurred on 4 April 1800: "The music of 'The Creation' has never pleased me so much, although not more than nine instruments were employed, and amongst them not a single wind instrument. Frau von Schönfeld sang like an angel, Reitmeyer very well, and Prince Lobkowicz expressively despite his thin tone. I stayed on for supper with Lobkowicz, the Princes Schwarzenberg and Clary, the Russian Ambassador and many other people."

In 1828, following the collapse of the Fries bank, the palais fell into the hands of Baron Simon von Sinna. Then, in 1842, it was acquired by the family of the Counts Pallavicini, who live there today.

A detail of the portal's caryatids.

opposite, above, and below: The ballroom in the Palais Fries-Pallavicini, with its luxuriant neo-Rococo décor, continues to be the setting of many festive occasions.

page 104: The staircase in the Palais Fries-Pallavicini as renovated in the second half of the 19th century.
page 105: The Red Salon.

The Albertina

It was the Portuguese Count Manuel Teles da Silva-Tarouca, adviser and minister to Empress Maria Theresia, who had this palais built in 1745-47 next to the Augustinian monastery on a section of Vienna's ancient fortifications. But even before the end of Maria Theresia's reign, the mansion came into use as a guest house for the court. In 1794, Emperor Franz II gave the palais to his aunt, the Archduchess Marie Christine, one of Maria Theresia's many daughters, and her husband, Duke Albert von Sachsen-Teschen. Just returned to Vienna from Brussels, where he had served as Governor-General of the Austrian Netherlands, the Duke began drawing up plans to extend and adapt the building to satisfy its new role as a princely residence and a gallery for his already notable collection of art. To execute them, he recruited Louis de Montoyer, who had worked for the Sachsen-Teschens on Laeken Castle near Brussels. But scarcely had work got underway when it was interrupted by the Duke's military duties as well as by adverse circumstances, both the consequence of the Napoleonic wars. Thus, only in 1801-04 did the new palais come into being, after Marie Christine's death.

As housing for the collections, Montoyer appropriated the third floor of the adjacent Augustinian monastery, today's "Old Albertina." True to tradition and the surroundings, he then articulated the façade in the language of classicism but with a monumental, architectonic accent altogether new in Vienna.

Duke Albert died in 1822, outliving his wife by 24 years. Throughout this period he devoted himself exclusively to the art collection, which the artistically aware and gifted Marie Christine had done much to initiate. The Duke's adoptive son and heir, Archduke Karl, had the interior refurbished by Josef Kornhäusel, who created the oval Minerva Hall with its statues of Pallas Athena, the colonnaded vestibule, the staircase guarded by sphinxes, and the ballroom with its two-color marble cladding and Joseph Klieber's statues of Apollo and the Nine Muses.

A few of the splendid interiors have been preserved largely intact, among them the Gold Room, the sheer luxury of which – equal to the Baroque at its most ostentatious – brings the ducal suite to its climax. In 1832 Franz Xaver Ritter von Sickingen described it thus: "This last room is called 'The Gold Room' with full justice because from the top, including the ceiling, to the bottom there is nothing to see but plain golden walls and suchlike panels, mouldings and ornaments with which alternate a variety of colourful paintings of both flowers and figures on gold grounds and many mirrors – which multiply a thousand-fold the already great opulence of this splendour – and give this room an amazing appearance that is further enhanced by two ottomans with heavy, totally genuine Persian cloth embroidered with gold and silver and by the floor, which is very artistically inlaid with pure rosewood."

In 1867, the façades of the Albertina were restyled in the historicist manner then fashionable. In the 1950s, the building underwent substantial alterations, a campaign of reconstruction that also repaired heavy damage wrought during the war. In

1899, the equestrian statue by Kaspar von Zumbusch was erected in memory of Archduke Albrecht, the son of Archduke Karl.

The Albertina's world-famous collection of graphic art, the largest and most important of its kind, resulted from the systematic way in which Duke Albert went about assembling art. Archdukes Karl and Albrecht both added to the holdings. When the monarchy ended, the Albertina's graphics were combined with the Imperial collection of engravings, which initially had been formed by Prince Eugene.

page 109: Duke Albert von Sachsen-Teschen, executed around 1770 by an unknown court painter (Albertina).

*The severely Neoclassical colonnade
with the adjoining staircase.*

*The Empire salons provide a
splendid setting for the Albertina's
collection of graphic art.*

*Two of the Muses by Joseph Klieber
in the ballroom.*

Palais Modena

On this site originally stood four gabled houses that little by little, through various campaigns of reconstruction, had to make way for or be absorbed into new building. This went on until the second half of the 17th century, when the Baroque Palais Dietrichstein had been completed as a single, self-contained complex.

In 1811, the Archduchess Maria Beatrix, Maria Theresia's daughter-in-law, mother of the future Empress Ludovica, and heiress to the ducal throne of Modena, acquired the property for 184,000 gulden. The new owner promptly had the Baroque palais rebuilt in the Neoclassical style, but retained its overall form, including the eighteen sets of windows, or bays, and the two entrance portals. However, the façade was completely revised to replace its Baroque exuberance and verticality with sober Neoclassical demeanor and horizontality; this shift in emphasis was reinforced by strongly projecting stringcourses, a band of Greek meander, and an uninterrupted row of triangular pediments over the windows of the piano nobile. The façades of the two lateral sections were crowned with pediments and balustraded balconies hung above the portals. The colossal series of pilasters, albeit retained from the Baroque palais, were radically simplified.

The plans identify the author of the rebuilt mansion as the "archducal architect" Alois Pichl, not Giacomo Quarenghi, who, thanks to the recommendation of Winckelmann's friend, Reifenstein, went to the court of Catherine the Great and won renown for his monumental buildings in St. Petersburg. However, Quarenghi very likely did have a decisive influence on Pichl and his work. For instance, Quarenghi's model, Palladio, and his love of Classical antiquity are powerfully reflected in the design of the great state rooms, which must be counted among the most important Neoclassical interiors in Vienna. The appointments throughout the interior – where the ancient deities reign in paintings and sculptures alike – are of the finest quality and elegance.

At the death of Archduchess Maria Beatrix in 1829 the palais devolved upon her son, Archduke Franz, Duke of Modena. In 1842 it was acquired by the state. From 1920 through 1923 the mansion served as the headquarters of the combined

overleaf: *The salons and the ballroom are among the most beautiful Neoclassical interiors in Vienna.*

Ministries of Education and the Interior. Today the Palais Modena houses the Federal Ministry of the Interior.

The exquisite stucco decorations in the "Octagon."

115

Palais Coburg

It was Duke Ferdinand von Sachsen-Coburg-Kohary who had Palais Coburg built in 1843-45 from plans prepared by Karl Schleps and Adolph Korompay. Not only the date but also the relative discretion of the façade, in both décor and articulation, place the great house within the transitional period between late Biedermeier and neo-

Romantic historicism. However, sheer size makes the structure atypical of its time, even though an authentic expression of the owner's desire for ostentation. Finally, Palais Coburg proved to be a bit too much, for within a few years the Duke found himself obliged to divide his magnificent feudal residence into income-producing flats. Because of the inauspicious moment for large-scale building, Palais Coburg caused a sensation in Vienna, much of it enthusiastic. According to the Österreichische Beobachter (1846): "This entirely new-built palais occupies a splendid site on Wasserkunst-Bastei with a delightful view of the hills. Work on the building has not been completed, but already [the palais] surprises the observer by its artistic and grandiose execution and by its very great splendour and solidity. The architect of this work, who has already presented the capital with many other similarly grand and beautiful buildings, is called Corombei."

Before granting permission for the new palais, the Vienna planning authority insisted on reviewing a painted model of the façades scaled 1:1. The task of preparing the model fell to the celebrated stage-set painter Michael Myr.

When completed, the signature tiers of columns could be seen from afar, thanks to the location of the palais on top of the old rampart. This, in addition to the slenderness of the columns, made the great house popularly known as "Fort Asparagus." The attic and its statues were added in 1864, at the same time that the garden had to be redesigned following the removal of Vienna's ring of fortifications. The official easement granting the palais' owner an unobstructed view over Stadtpark could not, however, prevent the construction of intervening hotel blocks in the second half of the 20th century.

opposite far left: A view over Palais Coburg and central Vienna.
opposite right: The grand staircase at Palais Coburg.

The monumental garden façade of Palais Coburg overlooking Ringstrasse.

119

Garden Palais

Favorita "Collegium Theresianum"

From as early as the 14th century, the site of the Imperial summer residence had been occupied by a dairy farm, which over the years could boast a number of owners, some of them aristocrats and some of them commoners. In 1615, Emperor Matthias acquired the property for the purpose of building a sum-mer estate, which soon made it known as the "Imperial Favorita." Around mid-century, Giovanni Battista Carlone laid out the splendid gardens – the real attraction of the retreat – and for a model drew generously upon the gardens at the Villa d'Este in Tivoli. In 1683, however, during the second Turkish siege, Ernst Rüdiger Count Starhemberg, who was in charge of defending Vienna, had Favorita burned down as a safety measure.

Emperor Leopold I decided to rebuild the garden palais, an undertaking that continued from 1687 to 1693. The architect is thought to have been Ludovico Burnacini in collaboration with Giovanni Tencala. Once again, the principal concern focused upon the gardens, which Jean Trehet designed, complete with such novelties as a theater, a grotto, and a tournament field. This reflected the Habsburg fascination not only with gardens but also with botany in general.

Under Leopold I, Favorita emerged as the cultural center of the Imperial capital, a place for concerts, magnificent opera performances, and other theatrical events. Here, almost any occasion could become the pretext for balls and festivities. When the Tsar of Russia paid a visit to Vienna, arrangements were promptly made at Favorita to stage the largest masked ball ever held anywhere. The palais itself, however, failed to inspire much respect or affection. A travel diary from the beginning of the 18th century notes: "When one hears of an imperial pleasure site one expects a place richly decorated with seemly luxury and selected works of art. But here one must alter one's anticipation for one sees nothing of all that but a long building, neither large nor high, and although some rooms are quite well furnished, there is nothing about the place that suggests it to be the pleasure palace of great emperor."

The topographist Johann Basilius Küchelbecker was not much impressed either, at least in his description: "The building is devoid of any magnificence, the stairs are narrow, the anterchambers rather small, and the rooms are furnished with hardly anything but a few 'tableaus'. Th imperial suite is nicely furnished, but modestly, without pomp or majesty."

Nonetheless, Emperor Karl VI fell quite thoroughly in love with Favorita. Indeed, it was here that he had himself proclaimed King of Spain; here that he prepared the Pragmatic Sanction, which allowed his daughter, Maria Theresia, to succeed him on the Imperial throne; and here, "in Wieden" as the district was called, that he died on 20 October 1740. By this time, both the palais and the garden had become a bit desolate. Upon the death of her father, Empress Maria Theresia gave the building to the Jesuits for the construction of a Seminarium Nobilium, whose current size dates from this time. After Emperor Josef II dissolved the school, Emperor Franz II had it reinstated as an educational institution and reopened in 1797 as the Collegium Theresianum.

page 122: An overdoor relief portrait of Emperor Karl VI surmounted by an allegorical figure of Fame.
page 123: The ceiling of the Gold Cabinet designed in 1724 by Claude Le Fort du Plessy.

The trompe-l'oeil perspective delineated in the garden gate is a masterpiece of Baroque wrought-iron grillework.

The extraordinarily long street façade.

above: The wall frescoes of Favorita's "Peregrine Hall" represent an allegory of virtues required of the mighty. The Jesuits then added the stucco work to symbolize the subjects they taught.

The 55-bay front along the street known as Favoritenstrasse – quite justly deemed the longest Baroque façade in Vienna – is highly unified, except for the central section, which was conceived as a great triumphal arch supported upon colossal Ionic pilasters and crowned by a triangular pediment, the latter emblazoned with the Imperial double-headed eagle. On the southern end of this vast stretch of masonry stands the so-called Oberer Stöckl, or "Little Upper Story," and at the northern end the former ballroom. Of the historic interiors, there remain the sala terrena, the chapel, and the Imperial apartments. Moreover, the old dancing room, or "Peregrine Hall" – whose precious frescoes were rediscovered and restored in 1983 – the library, and the Gold Cabinet figure among the most impressive Viennese interiors to survive from the 17th and 18th centuries.

At Favorita the tradition of higher education instigated by Empress Maria Theresia continues, as a college sponsored by the Stiftung Theresianische Akademie, or Theresianum, and also, since 1964, as the Diplomatic Academy.

Emperor Franz Stephan and Empress Maria Theresia, portrayed around 1750 and the Favorita library. Installed in 1746, the library may previously have served as an Imperial throne room.

The Liechtenstein Garden Palais

This palais, situated in the Rossau district, is one of the oldest aristocratic summer houses in Vienna. It is also a magnificent structure, whose interior and exterior have both been frequently imitated. Somewhat like the Liechtenstein town palais – built by the same architect although for a different client, Count Kaunitz – the Liechtenstein Garden Palais stands apart within the Viennese cityscape, thanks not only to its quality but also to its Italian characteristics.

The first mention of Domenico Martinelli as the architect occurred in 1689, when he was said to be working for Prince Johann Adam von Liechtenstein, a grandee known for his devotion to building. In 1691, however, Antonio Riva took charge of the project, only for the contract to be voided by reason of a protest from the local masons' guild, which resulted in the replacement of Riva by the Viennese court mason Lorenz Laher. Then, after several years of delay, Prince Liechtenstein engaged the services of another architect, Carlo Fontana, who proceeded to reconsider the plans from scratch. When his ideas failed to please, the patron decided to reinstate the original plans drawn up by Martinelli. He then hired Alexander Christiani to oversee construction, retaining Laher merely for the outbuildings. Finally, the palais stood completed in 1704.

For the interior, Prince Liechtenstein recruited the sculptor Giovanni Giuliani, the stuccoist Santino Bussi, and the painters Marcantonio Francescini and Michael Rottmayr. For the trompe-l'oeil ceiling in the Marble Hall, he also enjoyed the services of Fra Andrea Pozzo, one of the very greatest masters of Italian Baroque painting. According to the Liechtenstein archives, the artists each received twenty buckets of wine in addition to a generous fee.

The original complex of structures stood at the center of a largely unpopulated marshland, with the magnificent Baroque gardens stretching all the way to the Alser Brook, where a belvedere, designed by Johann Bernhard Fischer von Erlach, provided a climactic focal point. In 1814, the Baroque gardens were relandscaped as an informal, English park and a Neoclassical triumphal arch erected before the main building. In 1873, Heinrich von Ferstel replaced the beautiful belvedere with a princely house for widows, erected on axis with the palais and in the same style.

A quadrangular block of a building, the Liechtenstein Garden Palais stands three-stories high the entire length of its main front, while the façades on the garden front and side wings are so ordered about the entrance as to make the complex appear as if it consisted of a core mass with four outbuildings. The central section of the main façade, which projects only slightly from the rest, is taken up by the vestibule and Garden Hall. On either side, mirror-image staircases lead to the heart of the building, occupied by the resplendent Marble Hall. Here, the palatial décor comprises giant, engaged marble columns marching completely round the room, with the spaces between them given over to large oil paintings alternating with gilded Rococo reliefs. Above the cornice soars the glorious illusionism of Andrea Pozzo's Apotheosis of Hercules, painted between of 1704 and 1708.

Altogether, the Marble Hall in the Liechtensteins' garden palais survives as one of the most radiant triumphs of the Viennese High Baroque. Sheer artistic quality combines with an exceptional palette of colors to make the room a place of festive, even breathtaking splendor.

The Liechtensteins still own this garden palais, which has long housed a world-famous art collection, as well as a library and the family archives.

The splendid Marble Hall in the Liechtenstein Garden Palais epitomizes the Baroque in its synthesis of all the arts, including sculpture, painting, and stucco work as well as monumental architecture.

In the Marble Hall, Fra Andrea Pozzo's Apotheosis of Hercules soars illusionistically high into the pagan heavens.

In the Liechtenstein Garden Palais' sala terrena, intricately decorative stucco work serves as a frame surrounding illusionistic ceiling frescoes.

The semicircular outbuildings swing away from the main house to form a cour d'honneur.

133

Schloss Hetzendorf

Dating from 1684, Schloss Hetzendorf was erected for Count Sigismund von Thun as a hunting lodge, located just south of Schönbrunn Park. Johann Lukas von Hildebrandt may very well have drawn up the plans. By 1712, however, the palais had a new owner, Prince Anton Florian von Liechtenstein, who immediately launched upon a campaign of remodeling. Next, Count Anton Salm-Reifferscheidt took possession of the main building. Then came Empress Maris Theresia, who instructed the court architect Nikolaus Pacassi to adapt Hetzendorf as a home for her widowed mother, Dowager Empress Elisabeth Christine. And nowhere did Pacassi indulge his taste to better effect, especially in the decorative ensemble, which transformed Hetzendorf into something like a small-scale version of Schönbrunn. To create a cour d'honneur, he joined the elegantly proportioned main building to its lateral outbuildings. These, the service buildings, would however be constructed later during the reign of Josef II. Lorenzo Mattielli created not only the neo-antique statuary on the garden and main façades but also the stone sphinxes that stand guard at the side entrance to the cour d'honneur.

Important artists also worked on the interior, beginning with the vestibule, which features stucco work and the Aurora painted on the ceiling by Daniel Gran. Antonio Beuzzi's cycle of illusionistic wall and ceiling paintings in the ballroom are among the most remarkable examples of such High Baroque art in Vienna. Beautiful stucco work abounds in the gallery, while the Japanese Salon features sumptuous wood paneling embellished with soapstone reliefs and gilded Rococo flourishes. The vault over the chapel, built in 1745, was painted by Daniel Gran. In the garden behind the palace, a fragment of the original layout still survives. Schloss Hetzendorf now houses a municipal fashion school.

opposite above: The ballroom at
Schloss Hetzendorf.
opposite below: One of the sphinxes
guarding the side portal.

The central section of Schloss
Hetzendorf, clearly distinguished
from the wide wings.

overleaf: The Japanese Salon at Schloss Hetzendorf.

right: The gallery splendidly reflects the taste of the Maria Theresia period.
below: A detail of the wall fresco in the ballroom.

Schloss Schönbrunn

In the 14th century, a fortified mill – the "Katterburg" – stood upon the site of Schloss Schönbrunn and its park, which lies along the bank of the River Wien between the towns of Meidling and Hietzing. Consisting mainly of woods and meadows, the district belonged to the Monastery of Klosterneuburg. Development of the land commenced when Mayor Hermann Bayer of Vienna transformed the Katterburg into a manor house surrounded by a pleasure garden and vineyards. In 1569, Emperor Maximilian II acquired the property, for, like most Habsburgs, he was keen on botany and could not resist the Mayor's zoological, flower, and herb gardens. Then, at the outset of the 17th century, another Emperor, Matthias, is said to have discovered, while hunting, a "beautiful spring," or Schönbrunn, which accounts for the the name by which the area has subsequently been known. In 1637, the building there underwent renovation as a relatively sumptuous retreat for Eleonore of Gonzaga, the widow of Matthias' successor, Emperor Ferdinand II. During the siege of Vienna in 1683, this Schönbrunn was largely destroyed by the Ottoman Turks.

After the defeat of the Ottomans, Emperor Leopold I decided to build afresh at Schönbrunn, whereupon Johann Bernhard Fischer von Erlach, just back from Rome, drew up and submitted plans for a structure and site of extraordinary grandiosity. Five arcaded terraces would have led upwards to Schönbrunn Hill crowned by a palace of unprecedented dimensions. Very likely the young artist hoped to make himself known by the sheer ambition and complexity of his ideas, while also expressing sincere confidence in the scope and majesty of the Imperial House.

The Vieux-Laque Room at
Schönbrunn, designed by Isidor
Canevale in 1770.

below: The Blue Chinese Salon.
bottom: Illusionistic landscapes and
exotic, tropical flora decorate the
"Bergl Room," named for its creator,
Johann Bergl.

So colossal was the project, which bordered on megalomania, that it probably should not be taken seriously. In the siting of the palace as well as in its vastness and splendor, the design combined elements from the greatest palace architecture of the past with contemporary ones drawn from the clouds of an original, Utopian vision. Finally, a second, realistic proposal, which called for a garden palais of great elegance situated in the valley of the garden, was approved for construction in 1696. But scarcely had the central section been completed when work slowed and eventually ground to a halt, leaving the palace unfinished.

Schönbrunn, in fact, remained incomplete until the accession of Maria Theresia, who chose it as her summer residence. The new palace so pleased the Empress that she launched upon a lavish expansion of the original structure, a task undertaken by the architect Nikolaus Pacassi in the years 1743-49. Now cast in the role of Imperial summer residence and family home, Schönbrunn called for a fresh departure both inside and out.

Among the important new features were the Major and Minor Galleries as well as the Chinese Salons, which replaced the old ballroom. Meanwhile, the exterior would be altered by the introduction of a mezzanine floor. Fischer's splendid exterior terracing was interrupted and a new passage introduced leading from the cour d'honneur or forecourt through a colonnaded passage to the garden beyond.

Maria Theresia took a great interest in the furnishings, which accounts for the importance of chinoiserie, a favorite theme that proved especially successful in the so-called "Million Room." Here, the luxurious rosewood paneling is brightened by

260 Indo-Persian miniatures from the 16th and 17th centuries. Altogether, they offer a charming portrait of everyday life at the court of the Mogul Emperor. Other rooms are decorated with Chinese wallpaper or lacquer screens.

The Imperial family as a whole took part in fitting out the rest of the palace. The "Porcelain Room," for example, was so named because its walls appear to be sheathed in blue-and-white tiles, which in fact are ink drawings made by Emperor Franz I Stephan, the Consort of Maria Theresia, and their daughters Marie Christine and Maria Elisabeth, then pieced together, and finally varnished to sparkle like porcelain. A true monument to the cultural engagement of Maria Theresia's court is the palace theater, built from plans by Pacassi and opened in 1747. Located in the northwest corner of the courtyard, it was later remodeled by Johann Ferdinand Hetzendorf von Hohenberg.

In the mid-18th century the large gardens were laid out in the formal style perfected by André Le Néotre at Versailles. A start had been made earlier when Jean Trehet created a small garden that was already in place by the time Fischer von Erlach's original building was finished. The new garden featured the added attraction of a menagerie, which Jean Nicolas Jadot de Ville-Issey designed for Emperor Franz Stephan.

Jadot also laid out the "Crown Prince Garden" before the palace's eastern façade and the "Chamber Garden" before the western façade. Adrian van Steckhoven introduced the "Dutch Garden" in 1753, following it with the orangery in 1755.

opposite: The Gloriette on the highest point within the vast gardens at Schönbrunn.
above: A tree-lined avenue offers a perspective view of the central section of Schönbrunn's garden façade.

In 1768, the garden was expanded and beautified by Johann Ferdinand Hetzendorf von Hohenberg, who reconfigured Schönbrunn Hill so that the Gloriette could be erected upon it. Rather like a theatrical backdrop or a stage set, this "Temple of Fame," with its colonnades and trophies, was partly constructed with elements taken from the ruins of Neugebäude Castle, demolished at the time of the Turkish siege. The most interesting aspect in Hohenberg's garden scheme may be the mock "Roman Ruins," all perfect examples of the picturesque "follies" so beloved by the nascent Romantic period. Other new projects included the "Neptune Fountain," a sculptural group at the foot of the hill with figures carved by Franz Anton Zauner. In this part of the garden campaign, a significant role was played not only by Maria Theresia but also by her Chancellor, Prince Wenzel Anton von Kaunitz, who conceived the thematic program for the rich array of statuary.

Emperor Josef II, Maria Theresia's son, had scant affection for Schönbrunn and thus spent little time there. The last major renovation of the palace came in 1817-19 during the reign of Franz I, when the court architect Johann Aman made some minor alterations to the façade in the Neoclassical style. Pietro Nobile had proposed sweeping changes for the sake of a more unified style, but the Emperor rejected this idea.

Emperor Franz Joseph was born at Schönbrunn in 1830, and during his long reign, the palace would once again become the center of the Habsburg Empire. He not only made Schönbrunn his summer residence; he even spent a major part of the year there. In later life, Franz Joseph ruled the Empire almost entirely from Schönbrunn, where he died in 1916 at the height of World War I.

opposite above: The "Chamber Garden" laid out before the western façade of Schloss Schönbrunn.
below: The figure of a priestess by Johann Baptist Hagenauer in a garden allée at Schönbrunn.
below: The "Roman Ruins" in the gardens at Schönbrunn.

Augartenpalais

T he history of the "Augarten," a recreational area near the Danube, goes back to the late 16th century. But not until 1677 did a Habsburg – Leopold I – acquire a garden palais there, purchasing it from the estates of the Trautson family. The property stood upon land turned marshy by the river, whose flooding had not yet been brought under control. Leopold ordered the palais enlarged and the garden extended, only for both to be destroyed in 1683 by the Turks.

The Augarten came into its own again during the reign of Karl VI (1711-40), who had Jean Trehet lay the Imperial gardens out in the French style. With this, they became popular as a place of summer celebration, for both the Imperial house and the high nobility, despite their being besieged anew, this time by gnats rather than Turks.

Josef II was especially fond of the Augartenpalais, to which he added the nearby Palais Leeb, built in the 17th century from plans by Johann Bernhard Fischer von Erlach. The Emperor had the garden renovated in the contemporary manner, which meant vast lawns sectioned by long tree-lined avenues or "perspectives." His decision to plant mature trees was something of a novelty in Vienna, but it reflected one of the reformer-monarch's mottoes: "In everything which I have ever done in my life, I always wanted to see the final effect right away. When I had the Augarten and the Prater redesigned, I didn't want to work with young shoots, which would not be enjoyed in my lifetime.

No, I took mature trees so that I and my fellow men could sit in their shade from the very beginning."

Josef II commissioned Isidor Canevale to build Josefsstöckl, a simple summer residence that came into being in the years 1781-83. Its small garden would be one of the very first informal English park-gardens in Vienna, a modest patch of green reserved exclusively for the Emperor's own pleasure. As for the rest of the Imperial Augarten, Josef II had already turned it over to the public in 1775. Here, the entrance gate by Canevale is inscribed thus: "Dedicated to all People by their Patron for their Pleasure." On opening day, the court declared: "Everything is allowed which a reasonable police force would sanction and all those things which otherwise take place in public dance halls and parks." Everyone was welcome except "female persons with trailing bonnets and corsets and servants in livery."

The Viennese flocked to the famous morning concerts, inaugurated in 1772 and held in a garden pavilion built on the site of the former Palais Trautson. Mozart, Beethoven, and Schubert all performed there. Today, the building houses the Augarten Porcelain Factory.

In 1867, Josef II's Augartenpalais became the residence of the Comptroller of the Imperial Household, Prince Konstantin zu Hohenlohe-Schillingsfürst. The festivities the Prince staged there, with the Imperial family, the aristocracy, and a great many artists in attendance, were the social events of their day in Vienna. The palais acquired an additional floor in 1897, during its renovation as a home for the family of Franz Joseph's brother, Archduke Otto.

Since 1948, the Augartenpalais has been the boarding school of the Vienna Choir Boys. Despite numerous remodelings, the old Baroque building still retains its original sweeping staircase and domed oval hall.

below: The graceful, sweeping reverse curves of the staircase leading to the domed oval hall.

below: One of the richly furnished salons in the Augartenpalais.

Palais Schwarzenberg

rom this great mansion, one can still gain a reasonably accurate impression of what a Baroque garden palais was at a time when Vienna could boast many such dwellings. Most of the surviving country houses have essentially lost their original form as well as their coherence, which vanished once the gardens had been destroyed. At the Palais Schwarzenberg, however, the garden survives, albeit not in its Baroque design, but rather in the informal style of the English park. Yet, despite these alterations, the palais still conveys the feeling of a summery Buen Retiro in the midst of a metropolis. Thanks to the preservation of its terraces, reflecting pool, and statuary, the Palais Schwarzenberg remains surprisingly faithful to the intentions of the original garden architect.

On 3 October 1697, the Imperial Seneschal, Heinrich Franz Count von Mansfeld, Prince von Fondi, acquired "three sections of vineyard in Lampelsbrunn" from the Jesuits. He then commissioned Johann Lukas von Hildebrandt to build a summer palais on the property, and Jean Trehent to create a garden around it. As a consequence, the palais and the garden evolved simultaneously, as a total concept. Equally important from the start, the two aspects of the Palais Schwarzenberg arose from the single desire for a unified recreational area, whether the inhabitants found themselves under the blue of frescoed sky effects or the blue of the actual summer heavens.

Count Heinrich died in 1715, leaving the unfinished palais to be sold for 50,000 gulden to Prince Adam Franz von Schwarzenberg, who replaced Hildebrandt with Johann Bernhard Fischer von Erlach. After this architect died, his son, Joseph Emanuel, took over in 1728 and completed the domed hall and central section of the façade, which together had been Johann Bernard's assignment. Then, by the mid-18th century, the total garden palais stood whole and complete, with its riding school and the orangery contributed by Andrea Altomonte.

The rectangular palais joins with its twin outbuildings, symmetrically placed to the left and right of the entrance façade, to form a cour d'honneur. From there sweeping ramps lead to the triple-arcaded porch, which in turn opens into an oval hall crowned by a dome. The importance of this central section derives from the original plans drawn up by Fischer von Erlach the elder, who evidently conceived the palais as a complex of independent, self-sufficient parts. The statues envisioned for the attic front were never completed, the state of "unfinishedness" dramatized by the absence of capitals at the summit of pilasters.

The interior, including the domed hall, the main gallery, and the chapel, are masterpieces of sumptuous Baroque décor. The elaborate stucco work was done by the brothers Johann and Balthasar Hagenmüller and the magnificent ceiling frescoes by Daniel Gran. Unfortunately, a bomb dropped during World War II destroyed the painted ceiling that originally graced the domed hall.

The Schwarzenbergs still own the palais, using it both as a family residence and as a hotel/restaurant.

The ceilings over the chapel (left)
and the domed hall (right) are
virtually perfect in the taut
curvilinearity and white/gold
harmony of their décor.

page 153: The domed hall.

155

left and opposite: For the décor of the marble gallery, the full repertoire of Baroque devices was brought into play.

below: The garden façade of the Palais Schwarzenberg.

156

*One of the sculpture groups prepared
for the garden by Lorenzo Matielli.*

159

Palais Strozzi

In 1702, the widowed Countess Maria Katharina Strozzi had a small summer palais built in the large garden area lying just outside the city. The plans may have been prepared by Johann Lukas von Hildebrandt. The unusually tall and squarish central section was approached by way of double, curving stairs and flanked by a pair of two-story lateral wings. The appearance of the original palais is known from a description written in 1704. Among other things, the document mentions "... a very new and most properly built pleasure dwelling or garden house with a most comely façade. It moreover boasts a precious stone staircase, double in construction and a fountain from which water springs. ..."

At her death Countess Strozzi left the palais to her nephew, Johann Ludwig Count von Khevenhüller, who in turn sold it in 1716 to the Archbishop of Valencia, Antonio Francesco Folco de Cardona. Having come to Vienna in the entourage of Karl VI, the Spanish prelate left his palais to the Emperor in 1724. Empress Maria Theresia gave it to Count Karl Chotek in 1753 in recognition of his services to the crown. During the 1830s, the painter Friedrich Amerling lived in one of the lateral wings. Since 1840, the Palais Strozzi has been owned by the state. At one time it housed the Imperial and Royal School for Girls, and now belongs to the Ministry of Finance.

In the mid-18th century, the Palais Strozzi was given an additional floor, which automatically changed the roof line, thereby robbing the mansion, somewhat, of its light, graceful garden-palais quality. After the building had been expanded by several bays and its façade simplified, an entrance wing was added on the Josefstädterstrasse, styled in the eclectic, historicist manner much in vogue at the end of the 19th century.

Despite many alterations, the Palais Strozzi still possesses something of its original Baroque character.

Palais Schönburg

Thanks to its ambient garden, this mansion still has the character of a small Baroque country house. However, the palais and garden now look quite different from their original state. When built – around 1705 for Count Thomas Gundacker Starhemberg from plans attributed to Johann Lukas von Hildebrandt – the side wings had only one story and were clearly dominated by the oval central section. In the 19th century a story was added to the wings and the roof line changed, although the central pavilion with its attic balustrade and figures remained untouched. The princely Schönburg-Hartenstein family, which took possession of the palais in 1841, altered all the interiors save that of the library.

Only a pair of stone sphinxes crowning the columns on either side of the entrance to the bit of remaining garden survive from the original Baroque landscape, whose extensive lawns, pools, and statue-lined allées once culminated in a large summer house on the south.

The courtyard façade (above) and the garden façade (opposite) of the Palais.

Palais Schönborn

In 1706, after Friedrich Karl Count von Schönborn was summoned to Vienna by Emperor Joseph I and appointed Imperial Vice-Chancellor, he acquired from Marshal Otto Ehrenreich Count von Abensperg-Traun the property known as "New Court" together with its attendant garden. Count Schönborn then engaged Johann Lukas von Hildebrandt and his project manager, Franz Jänggl, to adapt and enlarge the building. By 1725, the expansion had been achieved, following which the palais was restyled in the Neoclassical manner by, probably, Isidor Canevale. The central section with its rich ornamentation stands in marked contrast to the broad, quiet treatment of the façade on Laudongasse. Here, the portal is overhung by a wrought-iron balcony borne upon garland-draped volutes. The great pediment above bristles with the elaborate flourishes of the Schönborn arms.

Under Count Schönborn, who became Bishop of Bamberg and Würzburg in 1729, the palais acquired a renowned art collection, which, after the death of the collector, was transferred to the palais in Renngasse. The garden was equally famous, especially for its tulips, then very rare. Count Schönborn wrote his uncle an account of them: "To conclude, I must tell Your Prince-Electoral Grace how beautiful and copious the tulips are. I think I must already have sent 2,000 of them to court. . . . I hear that there is nothing finer in the world for quality and variety than the anemones and ranunculi which are now coming up in my garden."

After 1750 the Palais Schönborn was let to various noble families. In 1845 the actress Amalie Vogl, the wife of Baron Pasquilati, moved in and opened both an amateur theater – the Pasquilati Theater – and a drama school. In 1862 the town council took over and turned the garden into a public park. Since 1920 the mansion has been the home of the Austrian Museum of Folklore.

The street front with its fine portal and the colorful Schönborn arms.

The central pavilion of the garden façade.

opposite: The former "picture room" retains some of its original appointments.

The staircase with its elaborate stonework reflects the celebrated taste of the Schönborn family.

Palais Auersperg

In April 1700, the city of Vienna acquired from Hippolyte Marchese Malaspina the grounds of the former Rottenhof estate, which would become the Josefstadt quarter, today known as Vienna VIII. However, part of the Rottenhof land came into the possession of Count Ferdinand Karl von Weltz, through whose heirs it would eventually be owned by Marchese Hieronymus Capece di Rofrano, the grandee believed to have been responsible for the garden palais built or reconstructed there around 1710. Both Johann Bernhard Fischer von Erlach and Johann Lukas von Hildebrandt were involved in designing the mansion, but presumably it was Hildebrandt who drew up the original plans, while Fischer von Erlach prepared the alterations and additions subsequently carried out by the builder Johann Christian Neupauer in 1721.

In 1777, Philipp Count Kinsky acquired the palais, followed by Johann Adam Prince von Auersperg, Lord Chamberlain and Hereditary Military Governor of the Tyrol, who bought it in 1781, paying 70,000 gulden. The new owner restored the country house and redecorated it magnificently. He had Niccolo Rossi paint the ceiling in the ballroom, a trompe-l'oeil composition that has, unfortunately, not survived. Josef Karl Henrici created the stuccoes, while Johann David undertook the actual construction work. In 1885, Prince Vinzenz Auersperg put the great house through the most sweeping renovation of all, a campaign made necessary by the raising of the street level outside. Gangolph Kayser added a narrow but tall colonnaded portico to the central façade, at the same time that an extension of the south front deprived the building of its overall symmetry. Also in the 19th

century, the Baroque garden gave way to a romantic English park, just as contemporary taste had its effect on the interior. Yet, despite the many revisions, the Baroque garden palais remains clearly present, both within and without the Auspergs' family seat.

The Palais Auersperg has contributed substantially to Vienna's fame as the home of theater and opera. The builder's son, Peter Rofrano, who died young, was immortalized by Hugo von Hofmannsthal in the title character in Richard Strauss' celebrated opera Der Rosenkavalier. In the room called the Bauernfeindsaal, which originally belonged to the palais, a permanent theater was installed in the 1770s. During his tenure in the mansion, the music-loving Field Marshal Friedrich Wilhelm Duke of Sachsen-Hildburghausen made it the scene of brilliant soirées and concerts, which for a long time were conducted by the composer Christoph Willibald von Gluck. It was also here, in 1786, that Wolfgang Amadeus Mozart led a private performance of his opera Idomeneo. Socially, the palais came into its true glory under Prince Johann Adam Auersperg, the host of many grand receptions. In 1790, on the occasion of the triple wedding in the family of Emperor Leopold II, Prince Auersperg received everyone in Vienna who could boast either rank or name. According to the diary of Wenzel Müller, the manager of the Leopoldstädter Theater who took charge of the artistic arrangements for the reception: "On the 27th [December] we presented songs and dances at Prince Adam Auersperg's in the presence of members of the Imperial Court: the Emperor – Kings – Archdukes, etc., etc. Prince Auersperg gave the company 50 ducats to share." In 1791 the Prince commissioned Lorenzo da Ponte, Mozart's librettist, to arrange a particularly splendid entertainment for the King of Naples.

Now that the severe damage inflicted during World War II has been repaired, Palais Auersperg is once again the setting for balls and other festive events, thereby maintaining the old tradition.

In the 19th century, the salons and the oval ballroom were restyled in the Neoclassical manner.

Mythological scenes in a characteristic Neoclassical wall décor executed in grisaille.

opposite: The décor of the paneled loggia, like other parts of the Palais Auersperg, reveals influence from English sources.

Stone atlas at the foot the grand staircase.

Palais Trautson

In 1711 Johann Leopold Donat Count Trautson was elevated to the rank of Imperial Prince, in recognition of his high service to the crown during his tenure as Lord Chamberlain under both Joseph I and Karl VI. By this time he had already commissioned Johann Bernhard Fischer von Erlach

to build a great mansion that could serve as both a town palais and a garden palais, thanks to its situation at the edge of the city on a site known as Ulrich's Grounds. Work on the project seems to have got underway in 1710, with Christian Alexander Oedtl, "Imp. Court and Country Master Mason," in charge.

While the main façade, oriented towards the Imperial residence, leaves no doubt about the official status of the owner, the garden front has all the characteristics of a private villa suburbana. Right away contemporaries recognized Palais Trautson as an extraordinary building, one of Fischer von Erlach's most distinguished works and a masterpiece of the Viennese Baroque. According to Küchelbecher, writing at the time: "Amongst all secular buildings, the beautiful and magnificent Palais Trautson is famed as being not only very large but also an uncommon variety of architecture. The façade has a fine pediment supported by Corinthian pilasters, and above it on the roof stand a great many statues. . . ."

In the new palais, Count Trautson strove to create not so much a monument to his power and wealth as a work of timeless beauty, a beauty derived from the great models of the past, most notably the temples of the Classical world and the Late Renaissance villas of Andrea Palladio. From this historical repertoire, Fischer von Erlach developed a new, highly individual structure that Hans Sedlmayr has called "one of the noblest palaces in Europe."

Dominating the main façade is the assertively projected central section, its three bays crowned by a full-scale pediment. To the left and right of this triumphal arch extend the lateral wings, styled in a similar but more restrained manner.

The full length of the main façade, horizontality is emphasized, beginning with the ground floor, where rustication is limited to the grooved divisions between superposed layers or tiers of stone. Further, the triple-arcaded entrance spreads entirely across the central pavilion, albeit with the middle arch reinforced by flanking pairs of Tuscan columns supporting an overhead balustrade with figures set upon it at either end. The drama of the central pavilion continues on the piano nobile, where the tall, round-headed windows are crowned by canopies so large that they almost touch the sills of the windows on the mezzanine above. This rich ornamentation, together with that of the attic statuary, is formally integrated with the great tympanum relief representing the gods of Olympus. On the side wings as well, the mythological theme continues in the decorative pediments of the piano nobile.

The garden façade combined with the well-planned garden to form a world unto itself, both aesthetically and functionally coherent. Thus, with its Classical design, the palais' garden front carried on a tense dialogue not only with the garden but also with the facing orangery and a large pavilion. The

opposite: The ballroom in the Palais Trautson, with its colossal pilasters and gallery of Hungarian officer portraits dating from Imperial times.

page 174: The main façade of the Palais Trautson.
page 175: The grand staircase decorated with sphinxes and atlantes.
left: This portrait of a Hungarian grandee, like those in the ballroom on the facing page, survives from the time when the Palais Trautson served as headquarters for the Hungarian Guard.
below: The vestibule leading from the main entrance to the grand staircase.

sala terrena, giving access to the garden, is splendidly frescoed throughout, and one of the few rooms of its sort that have survived with their decorative programs intact. Meanwhile, the large ceremonial ballroom, with its giant pilasters, remains impressive but much altered from its original state.

In 1760, after the Trautson family had died out, Maria Theresia bought the palais for the Royal Hungarian Guard, which the Empress had just founded. The new purpose required that the garden be turned into a riding school and the orangery into stables. Meanwhile, the palais itself fell into decay, a process that continued until 1961, when the Austrian federal government restored and adapted it for use by the Ministry of Justice.

opposite and left: This completely frescoed room – the sala terrena at the Palais Trautson – counts among the very finest such ensembles in Vienna. The paintings were executed by Marcantonio Chiarini and Gaetano Fanti.

The garden façade of the Palais Trautson joins with the original Baroque garden to form a complete aesthetic unit.

The Belvedere

In 1693, Prince Eugene began assembling land along Rennweg for the purpose of erecting a garden palais. The city map published by Anguissola and Marinoni in 1706 shows the project in the state to which it had been brought by that year. Here, we see the palais as planned for construction on Rennweg, an idea finally realized in the somewhat different form of the Lower Belvedere. Meanwhile, at the opposite end of the long site, where the main building would later stand, the maps indicates merely a summer house, designed as both a focal point for the garden and a vantage point from the garden's highest elevation. Johann Lukas von Hildebrandt, who had been in Prince Eugene's service since 1702, was responsible for the overall project.

The years 1714-16 saw the erection of the Lower Belvedere, in which the structure of the rooms and the layout of the domestic quarters suggest that a decision had already been made to build the upper palais. The Lower Belvedere is a long, single-story edifice composed of a seven-bay central façade and two lateral wings terminating in corner pavilions. With its steep elevation, the pivotal, three-bay entrance pavilion is clearly emphasized, which makes the building more strongly articulated by its three separate roof lines than by the elements of its façade, where a series of like pilasters and floor-to-ceiling windows runs completely across the garden front. The French-style windows – small-mullioned but generously scaled – endow the building with much of its summer-house quality.

The tall central pavilion is given over entirely to the Marble Hall, which rises through two stories and extends across three bays. The stunning effect of the room derives from its décor of rich, reddish-brown marble, splendid stucco work, and the gold of the sham architecture painted on the walls. The last was executed by Marcantonio Chiarini and his son-in-law, Gaetano Fanti, who came from Bologna for the purpose. In 1716, Martino Altomonte painted the ceiling fresco, which allegorizes not only the victory won by Prince Eugene over the Turks at Peterwardein on 5 August of that year but also the honors thus bestowed upon the hero in the form of a sword and hat blessed by the Pope. Other equally brilliant rooms include the Prince's bedchamber, the Grotesque Room painted by Jonas Drentwett, the Marble Gallery with its statues of mythological figures carved by Domenico Parodi, and the Hall of Mirrors in which stands Balthasar Permoser's famous Apotheosis of Prince Eugene. Today the Lower Belvedere houses the Austrian Baroque Museum, and the former orangery the Museum of Austrian Medieval Art.

The Upper Belvedere, which emerged as the main part of the complex, was built in 1721-22, requiring less than two years to complete. In keeping with its purpose, which was to provide a setting for the most formal occasions, the Upper Belvedere constitutes the High Baroque at its most splendid, the masterpiece within the oeuvre of Hildebrandt and a major milestone in the universal history of Baroque art. From a distance, the edifice resting upon its dominant elevation resembles a monumental summer house, a fairy-tale mansion of

The Upper Belvedere looms above
the figurative sculptures decorating
the source of the cascade fountain.

almost immaterial, dream-like beauty despite the immensity of its actual dimensions. This effect is heightened by the animated diversity of the roof line and the extraordinary wealth of the ornamentation, especially the sculptures on the attic and the small-scale, even faceted features articulating the huge façade. Thanks to the individual character of their roofs, the wide central block, with its strongly projected middle section, the lower wings stretching left and right, and the octagonal corner pavilions resemble separate buildings. What binds them together is the unifying power of identical pilasters

marching across the long, extended front to form an aesthetic whole.

The sala terrena, with its vaults springing from four giant atlantes, originally opened onto the garden through five bays offering an unobstructed perspective upon the city in the distance. The adjoining staircase once gave onto the courtyard, and it still leads to the reddish-toned Marble Hall. Carlo Carlone's fresco on the big domed ceiling, framed by trompe-l'oeil architecture painted by Gaetone Fanti, narrates an allegory of Fame, who announces the everlasting celebrity of the palais' master. Throughout the mansion, Claude Le Fort du Plessy oversaw the décor, which has survived only in part. To realize the program, the painters Giacomo del Po and Francesco Solimena worked alongside Carlone and Fanti, while Santino Bussi carried out the stucco work.

The Belvedere still bears remarkable witness to the Baroque style of gardening, despite the severely reduced state of the statue population and the radical simplification of the garden's original layout. To create his Belvedere garden, Prince Eugene engaged the services of an internationally reputed specialist in Munich. This was Dominique Girard, Inspector of Gardens to the Prince-Elector Max-Emanuel of Bavaria, and a pupil of André Le Néotre, the architect of Louis XIV's fabled gardens at Versailles. The great success of Girard lay in his designing the garden to establish a direct relationship between the two facing structures, with each of them given full visual access to the garden, which in turn appears simultaneously oriented towards both. Thus, the garden is aesthetically or formally coherent from above as well as from below, yet creates a different effect from either end. It is divided into two sections:

the sunny, gently sloping upper part with two big parterres, and the lower level, whose shady thickets and maze evince the full panoply of Baroque invention. Stairs, ramps, and cascades overcome the variations or gradations of level. In the Upper Belvedere's courtyard, the unusually broad expanse of water makes the building appear all the more shimmering and evanescent. As Erika Neubauer wrote: "In the reflections architecture becomes a fata morgana dissolved into colors and moving lines. Dissolution and unexpectedness contrast greatly with the severity of the rest of the garden."

In 1752, Maria Theresia bought the palais from Prince Eugene's heirs. To celebrate the wedding of her youngest daughter, Marie Antoinette, to the Dauphin of France in 1770, the Empress made Belvedere the setting of the most splendid reception the great mansion had ever seen. Seven years later she had the Imperial collection of paintings transferred from the Stallburg to the Upper Belvedere. Ever

since its opening in the autumn of 1781, the gallery has been accessible to the public. In 1897, the Upper Belvedere became the residence of Archduke Franz Ferdinand, the heir to the throne. Today, Prince Eugene's garden palais houses an important collection of 19th- and 20th-century art, which, like the collection in the Lower Belvedere, is a branch of the Austrian National Gallery.

opposite: The lavish Baroque forms of the Upper Belvedere reflected in the mirror-like surface of the broad pool fountain.

right: A detail from the courtyard façade of the Upper Belvedere.

below: The staircase of the Upper Belvedere, with stuccoed wall reliefs narrating the life of Alexander the Great.

opposite and above: The Marble Hall in the Upper Belvedere, created exclusively for formal occasions. The ceiling fresco glorifies the triumphant career of Prince Eugene.

The massive atlantes from which spring the vaults of the sala terrena.

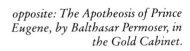
opposite: *The Apotheosis of Prince Eugene, by Balthasar Permoser, in the Gold Cabinet.*

The Grotesque Room (left) and the Marble Gallery (below) in the Lower Belvedere.

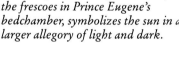

above: Apollo and Clythia, one of the frescoes in Prince Eugene's bedchamber, symbolizes the sun in a larger allegory of light and dark.

opposite: The Marble Hall in the Lower Belvedere with the statuary that originally adorned the Providence Fountain by Georg Raphael Donner.

Domenico Parodi's Diana in the Marble Gallery at the Lower Belvedere.

Palais
Rasumofsky

For his garden palais, the Russian Ambassador, Count (later Prince) Andrei Kyrilovich Rasumofsky, acquired so many plots and houses that his estate would stretch from Landstrasse to the Danube canal. This enormous site then provided a setting suitable for a palais meant to

connote prestige of the highest order. Konrad Rosenthal laid the entire area out as a landscaped English park, at the highest point of which Louis de Montoyer built the grandiose palais. When finished, the mansion would give Viennese Neoclassicism one of its authentic masterpieces. This mighty structure consists of the cubiform main building with an attached garden wing set perpendicular to it. Because of subsequent building on the site – which has spared only a small bit of the original park – and a raised ground level, the former sense of a great house on the hill has totally vanished.

The main building is articulated by pilasters on every façade, with the central section of each stressed either by a colonnaded portico or a recess. The colonnade on the garden side supports a balustraded balcony, the one facing Geusaugasse a triangular pediment emblazoned with the Rasumofsky arms in bold, elaborate relief. The vestibule – a colonnaded hall derived from Classical antiquity – leads into a circular hall with a domical ceiling. This room, with its sumptuous array of stucco decorations, provides the first climactic experience in what is an exceptionally splendid interior.

The ballroom at the center of the palais is one of Montoyer's most important works in Vienna. A giant colonnade running completely around the room close to the walls supports the high, coffered ceiling as if it were a baldachin. This chamber too suggests the interior of a Late Classical temple, at the same time that it echoes the ceremonial hall in the Hofburg, also designed by Montoyer. In keeping with the spirit of a garden palais, the ballroom seemed to draw the park within, as one guest explained: "There was dancing in the room, which has one open side giving a view over a beautiful part of the garden, which was brilliantly illuminated." While the ground floor, with its ballroom, marble halls, and domed room, was reserved for formal occasions, the upper floor housed the living quarters. A rare feature is the picturesquely decorated bar in the cellar.

During the Congress of Vienna, Palais Rasumofsky became the meeting place for a brilliant society. On New Year's Eve in 1814, the Prince gave a ball in honor of the Tsar, then in residence at the Hofburg. The celebration ended in a disastrous fire, which Mathias Perth described in his diary: "Because the fire bell was ringing nonstop, I rose about 6 in the morning in order to convince myself that this terrible thing was really happening. I hurried onto the wall near the Stubentor, where I encountered a great crowd and saw the dreadful drama, learnt the news, and persuaded myself that it really was Count Rasumofsky's palais then going up in flames. . . . The palais, so fine and so tastefully built, the splendid appointments in it – all suffered such damage that decades would not suffice to replace them. The most grievous loss is the Count's rich, well-chosen library, which was largely burnt up; also his beautiful and

193

The dome vault over the circular hall at the center of the Palais Rasumofsky.

rare horses, with a few exceptions, were consumed by the wrath of the fire. His Majesty, our Emperor, was at the site of this horror from half past six in the morning until the hour of noon. . . . Already for weeks the most tasteful, extravagant preparations had been under way for a big and, in its way, unique ball, which Count Rasumofsky planned to give in honour of the exalted monarchs. Now the [arrangements] are all destroyed, and today the ball came to a terrible end before it had even started. . . ."

It did indeed take some years before the damage was fully repaired. Even so, the garden wing, which had suffered most, would be restored only in a much-simplified form.

The Palais Rasumofsky also played an important role in Vienna's musical history. A great patron of music, Count Rasumofsky maintained his own string quartet and served as one of Beethoven's most generous patrons. It was in the Palais Rasumofsky that the great composer conducted the first performance of his Fifth Symphony. The tradition of music patronage was then continued by the mansion's next owner, Prince Johann von Liechtenstein, who cultivated a circle of the most important artists of his day. In 1851, Palais Rasumofsky became the headquarters of the Imperial (today Federal) Geological Institute.

opposite: The ballroom with its monumental colonnade is a jewel of Neoclassical architecture.

Palais Clam-Gallas

The Palais Clam-Gallas is an elegant Neoclassical structure with a simple façade whose central section is fronted by a temple-like portico. The mansion was built in 1834-35, from plans by Heinrich Koch, as a summer residence for Prince Franz Josef von Dietrichstein. In 1850, the Counts Clam-Gallas acquired the palais through marriage. Thereafter, in the second half of the 19th century, this Gartenpalais became a meeting place for the so-called "feudal nobility." Invitations to the many balls and soirées held there were very much sought

after and esteemed as marks of high distinction. The Russian Count Paul Vasili, writing in his memoirs, describes what it was like to be received by the Clam-Gallas: "One exchanges three words with a couple of friends, a conversation lasting ten minutes is interrupted twenty times, after which one goes home and asks whether it was worthwhile to dress up so finely and to put up with the discomforts of having to travel at walking pace in a line of carriages. However, one can recount that one was at the Clams – and that is enough!" The palais now houses the French Cultural Institute.

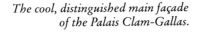

*The cool, distinguished main façade
of the Palais Clam-Gallas.*

Palais Metternich

In 1815, Prince Clemens Lothar Metternich had his villa in Rennweg built, and in 1846-48 he enhanced the property with a new palais erected in the garden from plans by the architects Johann Romano and August Schwendenwein. This building would have some art-historical importance, departing as it did from the usual principles of late Biedermeier Neoclassicism to embrace a new formal language, that of eclectic historicism, which produced a façade inspired by the 16th-century palazzi of Rome. The Palais Metternich must therefore be considered one of Vienna's first historicist works, even though it did not embody what would become the stylistic features typical of early historicism. The opulently neo-Rococo salons of the piano nobile have largely survived unaltered. In 1900, the palais gained a wing containing a great ballroom fitted out in an early Neoclassical manner and a music room modeled after Schönbrunn.

As Imperial Chancellor, Prince Metternich had largely defined Austrian politics during the first half of the 19th century. Thus, when revolution broke out in 1848, this powerful grandee had no choice but to go into exile. Only three and a half years later, at the age of seventy-seven, did he return to Vienna and his palais, where he would live until his death in 1859. In 1873, the Villa Metternich was demolished and the extensive gardens – all but a small remnant – divided up into building plots. Since 1908, the Palais Metternich has housed the Italian Embassy.

An enfilade on the piano nobile.

opposite: The salon (above) and the main façade (below) of the Palais Metternich.

The splendid ballroom in the Palais Metternich was inspired by local models.

The neo-Rococo music room at the Palais Metternich.

Ringstrasse Palais

Palais Todesco

In 1861-64, the Palais Todesco rose in Kärntnerstrasse on a site where the Old Kärntner Gate had stood before Vienna's ring of fortified walls came down. Ludwig van Förster and Theophil von Hansen designed the big, ostentatious structure for Eduard von Todesco, a leading Viennese banker. In keeping with palais tradition, the façades are dramatically extended, their horizontality emphasized by three sets of two-window bays and balustrades both above and below the piano nobile as well as along the attic, the latter supported by phalanxes of caryatids and crowned by vases. The modest scale of the abundant decoration reflects the nascent stage at which the architects and their patrons adopted the late 19th century's aesthetics of historicism.

On the interior, Theophil von Hansen clearly aimed for a Gesamtkunstwerk, with architecture, painting, sculpture, and crafts all treated in infinite detail yet fully integrated into an aesthetic whole. And nowhere did the architect realize his lofty ambition more completely than in the ballroom, where Carl Rahl and Gustav Gaul executed the paintings on the coffered ceiling.

Eduard von Todesco, a classic figure of the Ringstrasse period, discovered his genius for the stock market and became very rich, while also inviting ridicule for his love of foreign words and ignorance of how to use them correctly. But while Todesco typified the Ringstrasse Baron whose culture could not keep pace with his cultural pretensions, his clever wife Sophie, née Gomperz, won respect for her ability to hold the center of her own salon, where leading personalities from both politics and the arts successfully mixed. As a comment on the relationship between the Todescos and their guests Eduard von Bauernfeld composed this couplet: Jedes Licht hat seinen Schatten/Jede Frau hat ihren Gatten! ("Every light has its shade/ Every wife has her mate!"). Even Eduard Hanslick, the era's leading music critic, found that the women of the financial aristocracy – at least those who maintained salons – were "cultivated, with graceful manners and were receptive to everything beautiful." Moreover, "the masters of the houses were no trouble; it was enough if they were good-humoured and did not get involved very much."

Since 1947 Palais Todesco has been the headquarters of the Austrian Peoples' Party.

opposite: Details of the ceiling and
the doors in the ballroom.

The wealth of architectural detail
endows the piano nobile with special
importance in the overall effect of
the main façade.

opposite above: *The Judgment of Paris, a ceiling painting by Carl Rahl installed in the former dining room of Palais Todesco.*
opposite below: *A detail of the ceramic stove in the master bedchamber.*

The former grand ballroom in Palais Todesco.

Palais Württemberg

The architects Arnold von Zenetti and Heinrich Adam, with the collaboration of Carl Kayser for the interior, built this imposing palais on Kärntner Ring in 1863-65 for Duke Philipp von Württemberg and his wife, Archduchess Maria Theresia. The grandiose sculptural program spread over the huge crowning pediment and across the main portal (where it has been only partially preserved) was meant to leave no doubt about the owner's rank.

Be that as it may, financial circumstances soon obliged the bon-vivant Duke to sell his palais, which made it available for conversion into the Hotel Imperial in time for the International Exposition of 1873. In 1928, the hotel added two stories, which not only altered the building's overall proportions but also placed the pediment still farther from sight. On the interior, a few of the suites have retained their original neo-Rococo décor. The vaulted marble hall and the staircase, modeled on the court library in Munich, are particularly splendid.

The Marble Hall.

opposite above left: The family arms in the staircase of the Palais Württemberg.

opposite above right: The ceiling over the staircase.

opposite below left: Gold-ground paintings in the Marble Hall.

opposite below right: The staircase in the Palais Württemberg with its refined color scheme graduated from dark below to light above.

above: The salon in the Prince's Suite.

Palais Schey

In 1863-64, after acquiring a site at the corner of Goethegasse and Opernring, the banker Friedrich Baron Schey von Koromla had a palais built by the architectural partnership of Johann Romano and August Schwendenwein. A respected financier, Baron Schey was also a patron of the

Künstlerhaus and of the Musikverein as well as of the Museum of Art and Industry. Two of his favorite projects were the Academy of Commerce on Karlsplatz and the City Theater in Seilerstätte. At the latter, Baron Schey provided a work opportunity for Heinrich Laube, when this admired man of the theater was forced from his post as manager of the Burgtheater.

Palais Schey belongs to the "classical phase" of the Ringstrasse period, clearly evident in the pronounced, palazzo-like rustication of the two lower floors. This provides a solid base for the piano nobile above, which is further accented by the high-relief treatment of the windows, each with its ensemble of balustrade, flanking columns, and surmounting pediment. The wide-set, freestanding columns and overhanging balcony invest the entrance portal on Goethegasse with a strikingly spacious effect. The ostentation becomes ever-more pronounced inside, where the stucco décor of the grand staircase enunciates the formal vocabulary of the Baroque.

above: A detail of the entrance door.

Etched glass in the staircase.

The Roman palazzo façade of the Palais Schey typifies the classical phase in the new 19th-century mansions along the Ringstrasse.

Archduke Ludwig Viktor's Palais

Within the Schwarzenbergplatz development, which was planned as a whole, the first building to get underway was the palais designed by Heinrich von Ferstel for Archduke Ludwig Viktor, the Emperor's youngest son. It took six years to complete and cost 480,000 gulden. Not only did the Habsburg Prince play an important role in preparing his new town house, but a decision by a member of the Imperial family to reside outside the central area also did much to endow the Ringstrasse with the very prestige it needed for success.

Archduke Ludwig Viktor's Palais is an exceptionally impressive building whose creators clearly drew their stylistic vocabulary from the Italian Renaissance. The main façade lies upon the square, a straightforward arrangement that conceals the irregularity of a ground plan in which the acute angle formed by the intersection of Schubertring and Pestalozzigassse posed a problem, formally resolved through the device of a round tower capped by a dome. Obviously Italianate are the heavily rusticated lower walls and the pedimented windows of the piano nobile. Something special, however, is the broad and strongly projected central section, the whole treated like a portico with an arcaded and glazed upper story articulated by Corinthian pilasters serving as pediments for a series of statues. For the most part, the sculptures portray figures who once played significant roles in the history of the Habsburg dynasty: Niklas Count Salm, Ernst Rüdiger Count Starhemberg, Ernst Gideon von Laudon, Joseph von Sonnenfels, Johann Bernhard Fischer von Erlach, and Prince Eugene of Savoy. At the center, a pair of Classical caryatids flank the pedimented cartouche filled with the Imperial arms. Above this the façade concludes in an attic balustrade.

As would be expected in such a dwelling, the ambitious décor on the interior culminates in the grand staircase as well as in the state apartments of the piano nobile. These spaces provided a brilliant setting for the many festivities staged by the Archduke, about which Princess Nora Fugger has left an eye-witness account: "Archduke Ludwig Viktor, the youngest of the brothers, was a very peculiar personality. A witty diplomat said of him that he was a Seladon, a king of madrigals, a prince of the dance. This characterization is not bad if you add that Archduke Ludwig Viktor did not dance himself, but simply liked to watch. He was fundamentally different from his brothers, knowledgeable in neither military nor artistic matters, sickly, unmanly, foppish, and of a nasty exterior. He led a very worldly life, was informed – not always accurately – about everything, his tongue as sharp as a viper's. . . . In his palais on Schwarzenbergplatz he gave several balls every carnival season, often big dinners too. He was very choosy about his invitations. There were families he did not invite on principle, not because they had done anything wrong but simply because he did not like them."

Franz Joseph finally banished his brother to Schloss Klessheim near Salzburg, once the scandals surrounding him grew out of control. In 1910, the Emperor transferred the palais to the Casino and Military Science Association. Today the mansion

The vaults springing from slender columns in the vestibule of the Archduke Ludwig Viktor's Palais.

opposite: The main staircase based on Renaissance prototypes.

continues to serve as the headquarters of the Neustadt Officers' Association. Meanwhile, it is also used by the Burgtheater as a rehearsal space as well as the "Third Space" for experimental productions.

A salon on the piano nobile.

Archduke Wilhelm's Palais

Within the world of private Ringstrasse architecture, the pinnacle of achievement may have been reached in Archduke Wilhelm's Palais, a magnificent mansion sometimes called the Palais of the Germanic Order. Theophil von Hansen created this masterpiece, which came into being from 1864 to 1868. Two years after its completion, the house passed to the Germanic Order whose Grand Master was Archduke Wilhelm.

On the main façade the triple-arcaded portal stands tall enough to rise through both ground and mezzanine floors, whose smooth but deeply rusticated exterior walls contrast with the elaborate elegance of the highly classicized piano nobile. Here, the five-bay central section, which stands slightly forward, is emphasized by an Ionic loggia, whose order continues in flat pilasters marching entirely across the long side wings. Above the loggia comes the upper mezzanine, with its richly carved reliefs, and above that a final attic story, its bays marked off by caryatids supporting a balustrade and another rank of statuary, these figures freestanding like finials. An elevation of flat lower floors thorough the fully articulated piano nobile to the sculpture-laden attic leaves the palais in a somewhat top-heavy state, a characteristic not uncommon in historicist architecture. The caryatids represent the Germanic Order's heralds, while the figures on the top balustrade portray High Masters of the Germanic Order.

The décor throughout the interior is outstanding, with the vast dining hall taking pride of place. Thanks to its colors and sumptuous materials, this room glows with a festive mood and an almost holy radiance. As everywhere in his work, Theophil van Hansen attempted to give Archduke Wilhelm a Gesamtkunstwerk in which even the smallest details, such as door handles and appliqués, would partake of an overriding conception. Since 1981, following a thorough restoration, the palais has served as the headquarters of the OPEC Fund for International Development.

The dining hall constitutes one of the masterpieces of Vienna's 19th-century historicist décor. (page 219)

A vaulted and marble-clad hall made from the former stables of Archduke Wilhelm's Palais.

The iron-and-glass-roofed inner courtyard at Archduke Wilhelm's Palais.

The main façade of Archduke Wilhelm's Palais on Ringstrasse.

Palais Larisch

The French Renaissance was the stylistic source exploited by the architects Eduard von der Null and August Sicard von Sicardsburg in the Ring palais they built in 1867-68 for Count Johann Larisch von Moennich, a great landowner as well as Imperial Finance Minister. On the main façade running along Johannesgasse, the slightly projecting central section is an especially well-composed showpiece of historicist reinvention. At the corner, the round tower also constitutes a free quotation from France's 16th-century architecture. The high quality of the design and its décor, both inside and out, make the Palais Larisch a key monument in Vienna's late-19th-century architecture. The oval form of the grand staircase represents an elegant solution to a problem of space, which allows the vestibule to overcome its small size and create an impression of amplitude.

In its overall plan, the Palais Larisch followed the classic form of the Ringstrasse period, which reserved the ground floor for offices and workrooms, the mezzanine for the master's apartments, the piano nobile for the reception rooms and the apartments of the lady of the house, and the upper floors for children, guests, and domestics, in addition to, perhaps, an apartment or two for letting.

The palais, with its distinguished façade, rises behind the pavilion of the River Wien Gate.

Palais Lützow

In building this palais for Count Carl von Lützow, the architect Karl von Hasenhauer created one of his best and most mature works. Finished in 1870, the mansion exemplifies the residential Ringstrasse palais designed essentially for the use of a single family. Thus, the one apartment for letting on the top floor had its own access staircase. Elsewhere, the splendid main staircase led directly to the salons of the piano nobile. On the façade Hasenauer reined in his usual appetite for ornament and took the classic form of the Italian Renaissance palazzo as his model. The result is a broad, strongly horizontal front of calm, noble monumentality, enhanced by the wide, spacious colonnade of the entrance portal and the sculptural relief of the aedicula windows on the piano nobile. Here, the central window, with its flanking colonnettes and surmounting pediment, is further graced by a crown of arms and reclining figures.

On the interior, the décor is equally restrained and distinguished, with overdoors that count among the finest examples of decorative painting in all of Vienna's historicist architecture.

In 1899, Prince Max Egon IV zu Fürstenberg acquired the Palais Lützow, but since 1937 it has been the headquarters of an insurance company.

One of the salons adorned with fine stucco work and wall paintings

Palais Epstein

On this site in the "most distinguished part of Ringstrasse" – near the Hofburg – the master plan called for the erection of a noblemen's casino, which, however, failed to materialize owing to the exceptionally high price of the plot. This simply made the property appear all the more desirable for the extremely rich banker Gustav Ritter von Epstein, who decided to build a palais there and recruited Theophil von Hansen to design it. Even while dealing with the many alterations requested by his client, Hansen managed to complete the project in 1870-73. For this architect, the massive cubic block is unusual, as is the continuous, unsectioned façade. However, he left his signature in the wealth of terra-cotta garlands and festoons, the lion-head keystones, and the serried ranks of caryatids along the attic story. Four colossal caryatids supporting a balustraded balcony transform the entrance portal into an appropriate piece of theater.

The piano nobile boasts superb interiors in the historicist mode, with ceiling paintings executed by Eduard Bitterlich and Christian Griepenkerl after sketches by Carl Rahl. Vincenz Pilz and Franz Melnitzky contributed the sculptural work.

The Epsteins had to sell their palais in 1883. Except for the years 1938-55, the mansion has housed offices of Vienna's Department of Education since 1922.

The main façade of the blocky palais and its caryatid entrance portal.

Overleaf: Details of an ornamental pilaster and a stuccoed ceiling, as well as a general view of the large reception room in the Palais Epstein.

The grand salon in which the lady of the house formerly received.

227

Palais Henckel-Donnersmarck

The palais built in 1871-72 for the Counts Henckel-Donnersmarck exemplifies the work of the Ringstrasse architects Johann Romano and August Schwendenwein. Within the subtle, elegant articulations of the façade are such fascinating details as the caryatids flanking the windows on the second story and the attic aedicula capped by the owner's monogram. On the interior, large ancestral portraits adorn the spacious staircase. Here as elsewhere in the mansion, the old nobility made its presence especially felt, perhaps because of the new nobility that generally surrounded it on Ringstrasse.

Edmund Count Zichy, one of the most popular personalities of the Ringstrasse period, lived in the Palais Henckel-Donnersmarck for a time. An enthusiastic promoter of both art and crafts, Count Zichy made the residence into something "more than a museum." Contemporaries described the collector as "a portly figure inclined to corpulence with a long, snow-white patriarchal beard, who has all the Viennese on his side. His delicate feeling for art as well as his general culture places the Count on a level above the commonplace. Zichy is a friend of the arts not in name only; he gives them active support."

above: In this refined façade is reflected the self-confident reserve of the old nobility.

Completely restored, the palais has found new life as a hotel. The neighboring Palais Leitenberger has also been converted into a hotel, even while preserving the essence of its historic quality.

The imposing staircase in the Palais Henckel-Donnersmarck.

The gallery of ancestral portraits in
the staircase at the Palais Henckel-
Donnersmarck.

On the piano nobile, a salon
converted into a public dining room.

Palais Ephrussi

The Palais Ephrussi differs from the other mansions along the Ringstrasse by virtue of its being part of a multibuilding complex. The overall block is, in some respects, symptomatic of the entire Ringstrasse development, for, despite its various owners, architects, and minor stylistic differences, the total structure possesses formal and aesthetic unity. Alongside Theophil von Hansen, Carl Tietz and Emil von Förster took part in designing the group of buildings.

Several of the important commissions executed by Hansen in Vienna resulted from his close contacts with Greece and well-established Greek families. These projects included the Palais Sina in Neuer Markt, now lost, and the Greek Orthodox Church of the Holy Trinity in Fleischmarkt. And it was for Ignaz Ritter von Ephrussi, a Viennese banker of Greek extraction, that Hansen built the palais on what today is Dr. Karl Leuger Ring.

Calm and compact, the structure is divided into three horizontal zones, beginning with the two rusticated ground floors and rising through the two main stories, their bays sectioned by flat pilasters set against unplastered brick walls, to a recessed attic story with gilded-iron railings and tower-like corners. Here, the pilasters have been replaced by terra-cotta caryatids coiffed by freestanding urns.

Because of their excellent state of preservation, the great rooms on the piano nobile give a clear sense of the lifestyle forged by affluent Ringstrasse society in its moment of glory. They also reflect Theophil von Hansen's genius for color used in a subtle, sensitive manner. Thus, the restrained tonality of the walls serves to make the splendor of the ceilings, with their coffer-framed paintings, seem all the richer and more colorful. Executed by Christian Griepenkerl, a pupil of Carl Rahl, the pictorial scenes all derive from Greek mythology.

Palais Ephrussi is now the headquarters of Casinos Austria AFG, which had the building thoroughly renovated a few years ago.

left and below: Painted by Christian Griepenkerl, the painted vignettes on the gilded ceilings in Palais Ephrussi contribute significantly to the kind decorative richness loved by Vienna's Ring Barons.

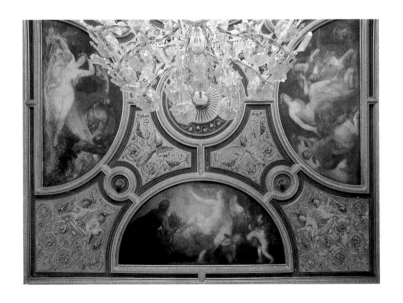

The façade of the Palais Ephrussi on the Ringstrasse.

*below and opposite: The interior
décor of the Palais Ephrussi climaxes
in the splendor of the coffered,
gilded, and painted ceilings.*

Palais Falkenstein

The architect Ludwig Richter, a pupil of Theophil von Hansen, joined with the contractor Alois Schuhmacher to build this palais in 1886-89 for Max Count Vrints zu Falkenstein. Not only did the Palais Falkenstein emerge as Richter's masterpiece, it also gave Baroque-revival historicism one of its most brilliant works. With this building, Viennese palais architecture arrived at its final, culminating burst of splendor.

The monumental central section, where the main and upper stories are bound together by giant engaged columns, indicates quite clearly that the Palais Falkenstein was modeled on French classical architecture. Atop the attic stands a sculpture group of Nike and her attendants backed by the mountainous rise of a Mansard roof or an Imperial dome.

Inside, a typically grand staircase opens into an upstairs loggia, which in turn leads into the rooms of the piano nobile, all richly decorated in a neo-Baroque style.

Today the Palais Falkenstein, located in Argentinierstrasse, houses the Greek Embassy.

A central section structured of monumental engaged columns ennobles and dominates the main façade

The grand staircase opening into an upstairs loggia (below), which in turn leads into a series of superbly decorated neo-Baroque reception rooms (opposite).

Palais Rothschild

Erected beyond the Ring, in the Belvedere quarter, this exceedingly grand residential palais was built by Ferdinand Fellner and Hermann Helmer in 1894 for Baron Albert von Rothschild. It was characteristic of the great, independent-minded banking family to have a private dwelling designed by architects known primarily for some other kind of building, such as theaters in the case of Fellmer and Helmer.

The mansion seen here is the only surviving Rothschild palais in Vienna, and its most striking features are the projecting central section of the main façade and the unplastered stone. All about the entrance portal, windows, and attic, the High Baroque reigns in full extravagant revival. The portal's massive arch surges up from the straining, muscle-bound atlantes to support a pair of urns in witty, calm repose.

Inside, friezes, wall paneling, and ceilings, all splendid in their neo-Rococo décor, join with the original furniture to provide a rare view of an intact, extremely luxurious late-historicist ensemble.

opposite: In both style and material, the façade of the Palais Rothschild reflects French prototypes, even while the entrance portal's muscle-bound atlantes adhere to a local tradition.

Here, Viennese salon architecture attained its final, climactic harmony. he plans drawn up by Semper and Hasenauer for a monumental Imperial forum on the Ring would be realized only in part.

The domed vestibule constitutes the pivotal center of the interior layout.

239

Picture Credits

Jacket: Palais Liechtenstein
End-papers: Panorama of Vienna by Gustav Veith, ca. 1873
Antiquariat Bourcy & Paulusch: 6, 13, 14
Bundesdenkmalamt Vienna: 9, 50
Johanna Fiegl: 204b
Historisches Museum, Vienna: end-papers, 15, 202-203
Kunsthistorisches Museum, Vienna: 17
Österreichische Nationalbibliothek, iconografic archive: 74b
Private collection the prince of Liechtenstein, Vaduz: 11, 120-121
Professor Gerhard Trumler: 142 (2) 143
All other photographs:
Wolfgang Kraus

Printed and bound in Italy

Litostampa Istituto Grafico - Gorle

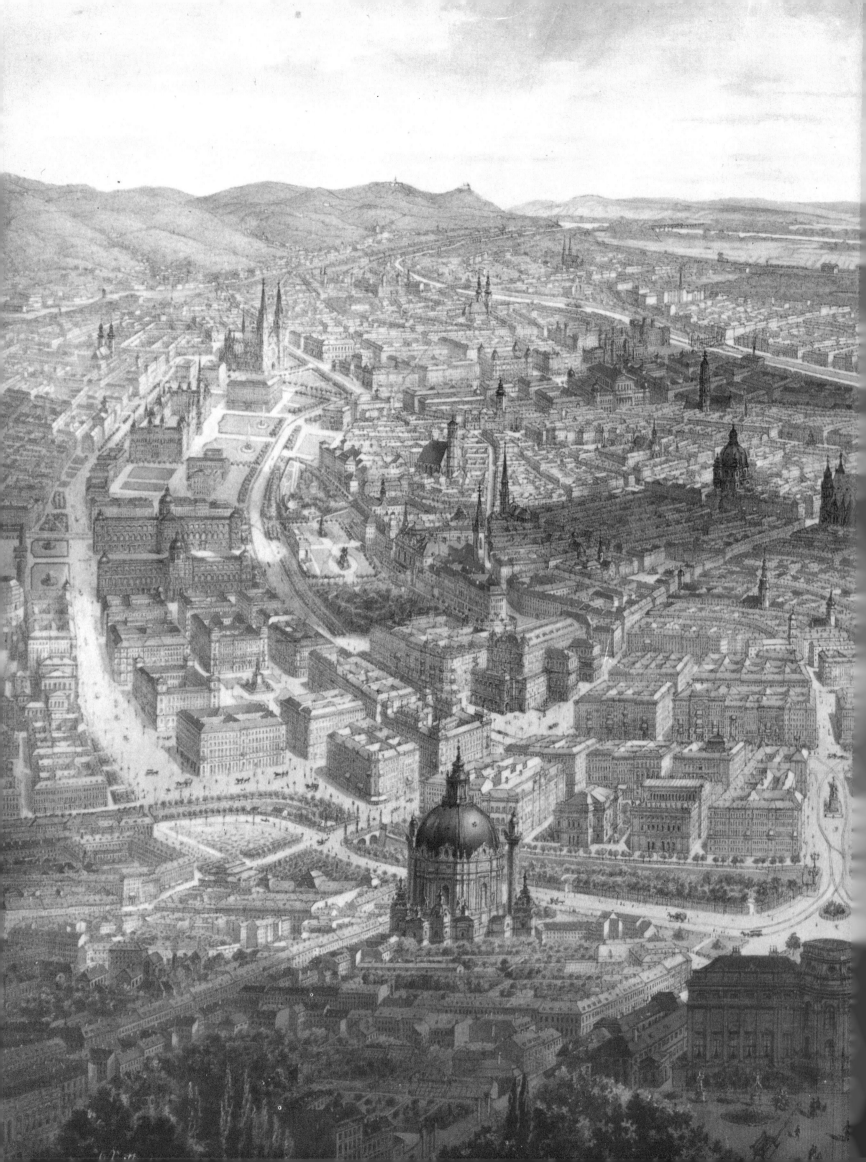